MW00800840

West's Law School Advisory Board

ADVOCACY CASE FILES

▪ ▪ ▪

By

Charles H. Rose III

Professor of Excellence in Trial Advocacy
Director, Center for Excellence in Advocacy
Stetson University College of Law

AMERICAN CASEBOOK SERIES®

WEST®
A Thomson Reuters business

Mat #41069115

610 Opperman Drive
St. Paul, MN 55123
1–800–313–9378

Printed in the United States of America

ISBN: 978–0–314–26818–1

Fundamental Trial Advocacy: The Law, the Skill & the Art

State v. Alexander

Cases and Materials

Charles H. Rose, III
Professor of Excellence in Trial Advocacy
Director, Center for Excellence in Advocacy
Stetson University College of Law

Notes

State v. Alexander

PROFESSOR CHARLES H. ROSE III
Director, Center for Excellence in Advocacy
Stetson University College of Law[1]

"We empower students to find within themselves their unique voices – to become the best possible advocates they can be."[2]

The following student at Stetson University College of Law gave of their time, expertise and creativity to assist in producing this case file. Without their help this project would still be an idea that was less than half way to completion. Each embodies the Stetson Spirit and I gratefully acknowledge their contributions. They are:

Center for Excellence in Advocacy Fellows

Vilma Martinez
Christian Radley
Allana Forté
Katherine Lambrose

Case File Project Volunteers

Jessica Austin
Jonathan Johnston
Ashley Mortimore
Jason Rice
Nichole Bibicoff
Lindsey Mack
Joseph Murray

I wish to express my gratitude to the leadership at Stetson - Dean Darby Dickerson, Associate Dean Ellen Podgor, and Associate Dean Jamie Fox. They helped make this text possible through their unfailing support of creative scholarship.

The ideas behind using case files to teach are grounded in concepts of experiential learning. It is in doing that true education occurs.[3] These files are designed to create optimal "learning by doing" opportunities – the foundation upon which advocacy instruction, if not all learning, rests.

---

[1] This work would not have been possible without the generous support of Stetson University College of Law's scholarship grant program for faculty.

[2] Professor Charles H. Rose III, Director, Center for Excellence in Advocacy, www.law.stetson.edu/excellence/advocacy

[3] Myles Horton, the co-founder of the Highlander Folk School, referred to this with a phrase from a Spanish song that translated reads "We make the road by walking." This is one of the best captured thoughts about experiential learning I have ever read.

– Introduction –

These case files are scalable, adaptable, and relevant to the issues facing 21st century advocates. They are based on the lessons learned by Stetson's faculty, students and alumni, reflecting the same commitment to excellence embodied in our Law School's award winning advocacy teams and national reputation in Advocacy.

A commitment to the law, the skill and the art of advocacy creates persuasive advocacy. The foundation begins with the ***process***: it's the way we train, the way we learn, and the way we practice. This is experiential learning. These case files focus the advocates on specific advocacy skills in a simulated real world environment, allowing participants to learn the skill and the law in the context of a moment in the trial. The exercises accompanying the case file develop advocacy ***skills*** through the rubric of the experiential learning process. This approach allows the advocate to develop ***values*** that contextually reflect the legal profession. These case files provide a structure for the ***process***, ***skills*** and ***values*** involved in becoming a better advocate.

The goal of this effort is to design a well-crafted, challenging case file that promotes excellence in all facets of advocacy instruction. The way in which a case file is organized, presented and supported is a balancing act that either increases or decreases its effectiveness. The result of this balancing act is a unique, multi-media product that provides both academics and the practicing bar with modular course content producing varied levels of difficulty (novice, intermediate, and advanced), that is developed for, and measured by, quantifiable outcome assessments.

State v. Alexander

CASE FILE CONTENTS

Tab A: Introduction......1

- Introduction to the Case
- Indictment
- Jury Instructions
- Verdict Form

Tab B: Police Investigations......17

- Officer Report of Incident – Alexander Murder
- Detective Investigative Report – Alexander Murder
    - Diagram of Alexander Neighborhood. Prepared by ABW
    - Diagram of Alexander home. Prepared by ABW
    - Diagram of Alexander home foyer. Prepared by ABW
    - Letter dated 5/15/20XX-2. Taken from jacket of Chris Alexander
    - Letter dates 6/1/20XX-2. Taken from jacket of Chris Alexander
    - Business Card taken from Chris Alexander's wallet
    - Photo of Wendy's bag of food. Taken by EM
    - Photo of bag found in Wendy's bag in Alexander home. Taken by ABW
    - Photo of baggie found in Wendy's bag in Alexander home. Taken by ABW
    - Photo of .45 pistol. Found in Alexander home by ABW
    - Photo of 9mm pistol. Produced by EM
    - Photo of exterior door of Alexander home. Taken by EM
    - Photo 1 of interior door of Alexander home. Taken by EM
    - Photo 2of interior door of Alexander home. Taken by EM
    - Photo 3 of interior door of Alexander home. Taken by EM
    - Photo 4 of interior door of Alexander home. Taken by EM
    - Photo of slugs removed from door frame by ABW
    - Photo of slugs taken from concrete floor by EM

- Photo of .45 ammo found in Alexander home. Taken by ABW
- Photo of skid marks outside of Alexander home. Taken by EM
- Shooting Club sign in sheet

- Officer Incident Report – Drug Activity

Tab C: Witness Statements..47

- Statement of Robert Hightower
- Statement of Nikki Long
- Statement of Sharon Barry
- Statement of Doris Presley
- Statement of Billy Bob Schifflett
- 2nd Statement of Nikki Long
- Statement of Anece Baxter-White
- Deposition of Roger Curlin
- Deposition of Dr. Jeremiah Jones
- Testimony of Brandi Alexander

Tab D: Reports & Certificates..79

- Chris Alexander Death Certificate
- Coroner's Report
- Chain of Custody documents
- Lab Report and Certificate
- PDQ Alarm System Report
- Cell Phone Record Report

Tab E: News Coverage..95

- Pelican Bay Star, Nov. 3, 20XX-2 "Doctor Horrible"
- Pelican Bay Star, Dec. 7, 20XX-2 "DA Argues Infidelity, Money Motivated Killing"

- Pelican Bay Star, Dec. 9, 20XX-2 "Detective: Suspect Lied Night of Husband's Death"
- Pelican Bay Star, Dec. 13, 20XX-2 "Teacher's Attorney Blasts Investigation: Defense Claims Detective Left Details Out of Report"
- Pelican Bay Star, Jan. 1, 20XX-1 "Teacher's Murder Trial Resumes"
- Pelican Bay Star, Jan. 4, 20XX-1 "Juror Dismissed in Ex-Teacher's Murder Trial"
- Pelican Bay Star, Jan. 9, 20XX-1 "Teacher Guilty!"
- Pelican Bay Star, Nov. 15, 20XX-1 "Retrial Set For Teacher Charged with Murder"

Tab F: Conviction Reports..**105**

- Chris Alexander Drug Conviction Record
- Nikki Long Filing False Police Report Conviction Record
- Nikki Long Possession Conviction Record

Notes

State v. Alexander

INTRODUCTION

Brandi Alexander was accused of the shooting and killing of her husband, Chris Alexander, on the night of June 6, 20XX-2. Chris Alexander, 32, was having multiple extramarital affairs and was allegedly talking on a cell phone with one of his lovers, a woman named Nikki Long, less than two minutes before he was shot to death in his living room. The Alexander's two children, Ariel and Jasmine, were asleep in a nearby bedroom at the time of their father's murder.

A gunshot residue test was performed on Brandi the night of the shooting. It found one particle of gunshot residue on the back of her left hand. The murder weapon was a .45 caliber pistol and has not been found. One neighbor heard gunshots but did not see a car fleeing, while another said she heard the screeching wheels of a car right after the shooting. The alleged motive for the murder is jealously, vengeance, and a $250,000 insurance policy. The defendant argued at the first trial that either an intruder, or possibly another jilted lover, killed Chris. Brandi Alexander was convicted on January 9, 20XX-1 and sentenced to life in prison.

Ten months later, the circuit court threw out her conviction and ordered a new trial, citing discrimination in the jury selection process by the prosecution.

IN THE CIRCUIT COURT OF THE FIRST JUDICIAL DISTRICT OF CALUSA COUNTY, XXXXX

STATE OF XXXXX,

v.

BRANDI ALEXANDER,

Defendant.

CASE NO.: 0318-20XX

INDICTMENT

I. MURDER FIRST DEGREE

IN THE NAME AND BY THE AUTHORITY OF THE STATE OF XXXXX:
The Grand Jurors of the State of XXXXX, duly called, impaneled, and sworn to inquire and true presentment make, in and for the body of the County of Calusa, upon their oaths, present that on or about the 3rd day of June, 20XX-2, within the County of Calusa, State of XXXXX, BRANDI ALEXANDER did unlawfully from a premeditated design to effect the death of a human being, kill and murder CHRISTOPHER ALEXANDER, a human being, by shooting him multiple times with a firearm, in violation of XXXXX Statute 118.01, to the evil example of all others in like cases offending and against the peace and dignity of the State of XXXXX.

A TRUE BILL:

George Peabody Smalley
Foreperson of the Grand Jury

I, Prosecutor for the Circuit Court in the First Judicial District, in and for Calusa County, XXXXX, do hereby aver, as authorized and required by law, that I have acted in an advisory capacity to the Grand Jurors of Calusa County previous to their returning the above indictment in the above-styled case.

Nick Cox
PROSECUTOR
FIRST JUDICIAL DISTRICT
CALUSA COUNTY

Presented before: the Honorable Jerry Parker, 1st Judicial Circuit, Calusa County, XXXXX

IN THE CIRCUIT COURT OF THE FIRST JUDICIAL DISTRICT OF CALUSA COUNTY, XXXXX

STATE OF XXXXX,

v.

DEFENDANT

JURY INTRUCTION NO.: 1

Plea of Not Guilty; Reasonable Doubt; and Burden of Proof

The defendant has entered a plea of not guilty. This means you must presume or believe the defendant is innocent. The presumption stays with the defendant as to each material allegation in the [information] [indictment] through each stage of the trial unless it has been overcome by the evidence to the exclusion of and beyond a reasonable doubt.

To overcome the defendant's presumption of innocence, the State has the burden of proving the crime with which the defendant is charged was committed and the defendant is the person who committed the crime.

The defendant is not required to present evidence or prove anything.

Whenever the words "reasonable doubt" are used you must consider the following:

A reasonable doubt is not a mere possible doubt, a speculative, imaginary or forced doubt. Such a doubt must not influence you to return a verdict of not guilty if you have an abiding conviction of guilt. On the other hand, if, after carefully considering, comparing and weighing all the evidence, there is not an abiding conviction of guilt, or, if, having a conviction, it is one which is not stable but one which wavers and vacillates, then the charge is not proved beyond every reasonable doubt and you must find the defendant not guilty because the doubt is reasonable.

It is to the evidence introduced in this trial, and to it alone, that you are to look for that proof.

A reasonable doubt as to the guilt of the defendant may arise from the evidence, conflict in the evidence, or the lack of evidence.

If you have a reasonable doubt, you should find the defendant not guilty. If you have no reasonable doubt, you should find the defendant guilty.

IN THE CIRCUIT COURT OF THE FIRST JUDICIAL DISTRICT OF CALUSA COUNTY, XXXXX

STATE OF XXXXX,

v.

DEFENDANT

JURY INTRUCTION NO.: 2

Murder — First Degree
§ 782.04(1)(A), Stat.

To prove the crime of First Degree Premeditated Murder, the State must prove the following three elements beyond a reasonable doubt:

1. (Victim) is dead.

2. The death was caused by the criminal act of (defendant).

3. There was a premeditated killing of (victim).

An "act" includes a series of related actions arising from and performed pursuant to a single design or purpose.

"Killing with premeditation" is killing after consciously deciding to do so. The decision must be present in the mind at the time of the killing. The law does not fix the exact period of time that must pass between the formation of the premeditated intent to kill and the killing. The period of time must be long enough to allow reflection by the defendant. The premeditated intent to kill must be formed before the killing.

The question of premeditation is a question of fact to be determined by you from the evidence. It will be sufficient proof of premeditation if the circumstances of the killing and the conduct of the accused convince you beyond a reasonable doubt of the existence of premeditation at the time of the killing.

IN THE CIRCUIT COURT OF THE FIRST JUDICIAL DISTRICT OF CALUSA COUNTY, XXXXX

STATE OF XXXXX,

v.

DEFENDANT

JURY INTRUCTION NO.: 3

Murder — Second Degree
§ 782.04(2), Stat.

To prove the crime of Second Degree Murder, the State must prove the following three elements beyond a reasonable doubt:

1. (Victim) is dead.
2. The death was caused by the criminal act of (defendant).
3. There was an unlawful killing of (victim) by an act imminently dangerous to another and demonstrating a depraved mind without regard for human life.

An "act" includes a series of related actions arising from and performed pursuant to a single design or purpose.

An act is "imminently dangerous to another and demonstrating a depraved mind" if it is an act or series of acts that:

1. a person of ordinary judgment would know is reasonably certain to kill or do serious bodily injury to another, and
2. is done from ill will, hatred, spite, or an evil intent, and
3. is of such a nature that the act itself indicates an indifference to human life.

In order to convict of Second Degree Murder, it is not necessary for the State to prove the defendant had an intent to cause death.

IN THE CIRCUIT COURT OF THE FIRST JUDICIAL DISTRICT OF CALUSA COUNTY, XXXXX

STATE OF XXXXX,

v.

DEFENDANT

JURY INTRUCTION NO.: 4

Weighing the Evidence

It is up to you to decide what evidence is reliable. You should use your common sense in deciding which is the best evidence, and which evidence should not be relied upon in considering your verdict. You may find some of the evidence not reliable, or less reliable than other evidence.

You should consider how the witnesses acted, as well as what they said. Some things you should consider are:

1. Did the witness seem to have an opportunity to see and know the things about which the witness testified?
2. Did the witness seem to have an accurate memory?
3. Was the witness honest and straightforward in answering the attorneys' questions?
4. Did the witness have some interest in how the case should be decided?
5. Does the witness's testimony agree with the other testimony and other evidence in the case?

IN THE CIRCUIT COURT OF THE FIRST JUDICIAL DISTRICT OF CALUSA COUNTY, XXXXX

STATE OF XXXXX,

v.

DEFENDANT

JURY INTRUCTION NO.: 5

Rules for Deliberation

These are some general rules that apply to your discussion. You must follow these rules in order to return a lawful verdict:

1. You must follow the law as it is set out in these instructions. If you fail to follow the law, your verdict will be a miscarriage of justice. There is no reason for failing to follow the law in this case. All of us are depending upon you to make a wise and legal decision in this matter.

2. This case must be decided only upon the evidence that you have heard from the testimony of the witnesses [and have seen in the form of the exhibits in evidence] and these instructions.

3. This case must not be decided for or against anyone because you feel sorry for anyone, or are angry at anyone.

4. Remember, the lawyers are not on trial. Your feelings about them should not influence your decision in this case.

5. Your verdict should not be influenced by feelings of prejudice, bias, or sympathy. Your verdict must be based on the evidence, and on the law contained in these instructions.

In closing, let me remind you that it is important that you follow the law spelled out in these instructions in deciding your verdict. There are no other laws that apply to this case. Even if you do not like the laws that must be applied, you must use them. For two centuries we have lived by the constitution and the law. No juror has the right to violate rules we all share.

IN THE CIRCUIT COURT OF TWENTIETH JUDICIAL DISTRICT
CALUSA COUNTY, XXXXX
CRIMINAL DIVISION
VERDICT FORM

State	)	
	)	
	)	CASE NO.: 20XX-**2-183**
v.	)	
	)	DIVISION:
	)	
Alexander.	)	
	)	

We, the Jury, return the following verdict, and each of us concerns in this verdict:
(Choose the appropriate verdict)

I. NOT GUILTY

We, the jury, find the defendant, Christopher Alexander, NOT GUILTY.

____
Foreperson

II. FIRST DEGREE MURDER

To prove the crime of First Degree Premeditated Murder, the State must prove the following three elements beyond a reasonable doubt:

1. (Victim) is dead.
2. The death was caused by the criminal act of (defendant).
3. There was a premeditated killing of (victim).

We, the jury, find the defendant, Christopher Alexander, GUILTY of Murder in the First Degree.

____
Foreperson

III. SECOND DEGREE MURDER

To prove the crime of Second Degree Murder, the State must prove the following three elements beyond a reasonable doubt:

1. (Victim) is dead.

2. The death was caused by the criminal act of (defendant).

3. There was an unlawful killing of (victim) by an act imminently dangerous to another and demonstrating a depraved mind without regard for human life.

We, the jury, find the defendant, Christopher Alexander, GUILTY of Murder in the Second Degree.

____
Foreperson

-Notes-

- 1st officer on scene could smell burning Rubber/Burnt rubber
- Arrived ~ 10 Min after being dispatched
- Fresh skid marks, no car
- Front door was open, lights in the house were on
- Shell casings outside the home
- Dead body on its back, woman appeared to be trying to "wake up" dead guy
- Body was shot in the groin

CALUSA POLICE DEPARTMENT
CALUSA COUNTY

INCIDENT REPORT
PAGE 1 OF 3

OFFICER'S NAME:	DATE:	TIME:	LOCATION:
A B-White	6-6-20XX-2	2301 hours	West Calusa Hills

COMPLAINANT'S NAME:	DOB:	ADDRESS:	CITY / STATE ZIP
PDQ Alarm Systems		6731 Lullaby Lane	Pelican Bay, XX 33707

HOME PHONE NUMBER:	WORK PHONE NUMBER:	MOBILE/PAGER NUMBER:
		n/a

ALLEGED SUSPECT'S NAME:	DOB:	ADDRESS:	CITY / STATE ZIP
Brandi Alexander		6731 Lullaby Lane	Pelican Bay, XX 33707

HOME PHONE NUMBER:	WORK PHONE NUMBER:	MOBILE/PAGER NUMBER:
555-5172	555-6382	555-3327

(W1) WITNESS'S NAME:	DOB:	ADDRESS:	CITY / STATE ZIP
Doris Presley	2-4-51	Lullaby Lane	Pelican Bay, XX 33707

HOME PHONE NUMBER:	WORK PHONE NUMBER:	MOBILE/PAGER NUMBER:

(W2) WITNESS'S NAME:	DOB:	ADDRESS:	CITY / STATE ZIP
Robert Hightower	10/31-64	Lullaby lance	Pelican Bay, XX 33707

HOME PHONE NUMBER:	WORK PHONE NUMBER:	MOBILE/PAGER NUMBER:
555-8442	555-0997	555-3997

WRITE COMPLETE DETAILED REPORT:

The department received a call at the station from an alarm service that was reporting a shooting at a home on Lullaby lane. I proceeded directly to the home, arriving in approximately 10 minutes. Upon arrival I observed that the front door was open with light on inside the home. Neighbors were gathered at the homes on both sides of the house in question, as well as in the front yards across the street. Upon approaching the house I noticed the smell of burning rubber and noted that there were skid marks that appeared to be fresh in front of the home on Lullaby lane, on the road itself.

OFFICER'S SIGNATURE	PRINTED NAME / RANK / BADGE NUMBER
Anece Baxter-White	Anece Baxter-White Patrolman #4613

Report Continued from Page 1:	

Lights were on in the home and the front door appeared open. I proceeded to the front door, identifying myself as a police officer. Upon arriving in the home I noticed shell casings on the ground outside and inside the front door. A woman was weeping uncontrollably while kneeling next to the body of a man – she appeared to be trying to wake him up.

I inspected the body laying in the foyer. It was clear that several shots had been fired into the body, specifically two shots or more to the groin. I noticed that there were several bullet holes in the floor underneath the body, and I found at least one bullet lodged in the door frame of the foyer. I also found two notes that are attached to this incident report in the pocket of the dead man, as well as a business card in his wallet.

Looking around the house I noted that the television was on very loud in the den next to the foyer. Upon entering the den I noted the presence of a Wendy's food bag. Inside the bag was a cheeseburger and fries. Underneath the cheeseburger I found 1 plastic bag of what appeared to be marijuana and an additional small bag of white powder. I conducted field tests and results indicated that the powder contained cocaine and the green leafy substance was marijuana. After speaking with the wife it was determined that a GSR test of her hands was not necessary. My team and I left after questioning the wife.
Upon arriving at the station instructed to return to the Alexander home to assist in additional investigation.

OFFICER'S SIGNATURE	PRINTED NAME / RANK / BADGE NUMBER
Anece Baxter-White	Anece Baxter-White/officer/#4613

INITIALS

ABW

Report Continued from Page 2:	

Returned to the home. Retrieved 6 remnants of slugs, 2 from the door jamb and 4 from the floor. Retrieved box of .45 caliber ammunition provided by Ms. Alexander. All evidence gathered was taken to the evidence room. Photos were forward to detective Edwin Morris, along with diagrams of the area.

---------------------------------Nothing Follows---------------------------------

OFFICER'S SIGNATURE	PRINTED NAME / RANK / BADGE NUMBER
Anece Baxter-White	Aneœ Baxter-White/officœr/#4613

REPORTING OFFICER Anece Baxter-White DATE REPORTED 6/6/20XX-2

	SIGNATURE	OFFICER BADGE	DATE
REPORTING OFFICER	Anece Baxter-White	#4613	6/7/20XX-2
REVIEWING SUPERVISOR	Willie Hightower	#1240	6/7/20XX-2

CALUSA POLICE DEPARTMENT
CALUSA COUNTY

REPORT OF INVESTIGATION
PAGE 1 OF 2

Report No	Date:	Complaining Witness:
20XX-206060321	6/8/20XX-02	PDQ Alarm Systems

Investigating Officer:	Suspect:
Detective Edwin Morris	Brandi Alexander (wife of decedent)
Division:	Address:
Homicide	6731 Lullabye Lane, Pelican Bay, XX 33707

Victim(s):	Age:	General Description:
Christopher Alexander	32	Male, 72", 195 lbs, Tattoo - Frostie

Investigator's Notes, June 8, 20XX-2:
Case assigned to Homicide division. Opened case file, began investigation.

On June 6, 20XX:-2 Officer Baxter-White and Chief Willie Hightower responded to a PDQ alarm system 911 call indicating an attack at the Alexander residence. Canvassed neighborhood for witnesses. Identified potential individuals to interview. She Prepared diagrams of neighborhood (exhibit 1), Alexander home (exhibit 2), and Interior of Alexander home (exhibit 3). Officer Baxter-White collected two letters from the coat pocket of the deceased (exhibit 4 &5), and a business card from the deceased's wallet (exhibit 6).

June 7, 20XX-2.
Developed diagrams of the relevant areas of Lullaby Lane (exhibit 1,2 and 3 of this report)
Catalogued & Photographed the following evidence seized from the Alexander Home:

- Bag of Wendy's food (exhibit 7)
- Bag of green leafy substance (probable marijuana)(exhibit 8)
- Bag of white powder (probable cocaine) (exhibit 9)
- Photograph of a .45 pistol (note this is a photograph found in the home on the writing desk of Ms. Alexander) (exhibit 10)
- Photograph of a 9mm pistol matching description of that owned by Chris Alexander (exhibit 11)
- Photographs of the bullet holes in the home(exhibits 12, 13, 14, 15, 16)
- Photographs of slugs and ammunition retrieved from Alexander home (exhibits 17, 18, 19)
- Photograph of tire marks on Lullaby Lane(exhibit 20)

June 18, 20XX-2.
Received Coroner's Report, inserted into case file

June 23, 20XX-2.
Visited "From My Cold Dead Hands" Gun Club. Retrieved Sign In Roster for May 25, 20XX-2 and inserted into case file.

July 4, 20XX-2.
Statement of Robert Hightower taken by Edwin Morris

CALUSA POLICE DEPARTMENT
CALUSA COUNTY

REPORT OF INVESTIGATION

July 8, 20XX-2
Statement of Ms. Nikki Long taken by Edwin Morris

August 12, 20XX-2.
Statement of Ms. Sharon Barry taken. Inserted into case file.
Received statement of Ms. Doris Presley taken by Investigator Stubbs. Inserted into case file.

August 14, 20XX-2.
Received statement of Billy Bob Schifflet taken by Investigator Stubbs. Inserted into case file.

August 15, 20XX-2
Received death certificate from coroner's office, inserted into file

September 23, 20XX-2
Inserted photo of 9mm pistol matching the description of the one owned by Chris Alexander (based upon the firearm registration records for said firearm)

October 10, 20XX-2.
Received results of drug testing. Inserted Lab report and chain of custody document into the file.

October 14, 20XX-2.
Recovered PDQ Alarm Report for month of June 20XX-2. Inserted into case file

Subsequent investigation revealed that Brandi Alexander shot and killed her husband, Chris Alexander, using a .45 caliber weapon. Investigative efforts included interviewing all identified witnesses, recovered evidence and searching for potential weapons registered to the Alexander's. Two weapons were registered to Chris Alexander, a .45 caliber pistol and a 9mm Beretta. I recovered a picture of the .45 registered to Chris Alexander. This picture was provided by Ms. Alexander in accordance with my request. Neither weapon was recovered at the scene. Through proper investigative steps I was able to ascertain that Ms. Alexander was familiar with the .45 caliber weapon, having fired it at the gun range approximately one week prior to the murder. Probable cause clearly exists Brandi Alexander murdered Chris Alexander. Forwarded contents of case file to state prosecutor on October 15, 20XX-2.

Investigation continues.
July 13, 20XX-1. Received affidavit of Officer Anece Baxter-White.
July 19, 20XX-1. Statement of Nikki Long taken by Edwin Morris at Ms. Long's request.

Investigation continues.

Sworn and subscribed in my presence, June 12, 2005. Signature: *Edwin Morris*	I swear and affirm that the report above and the attached files are true and correct to the best of my Belief and Knowledge.
Supervisor: Robert Burrell Supervisor's Signature *Robert Burrell*	Signature: *Edwin Morris*

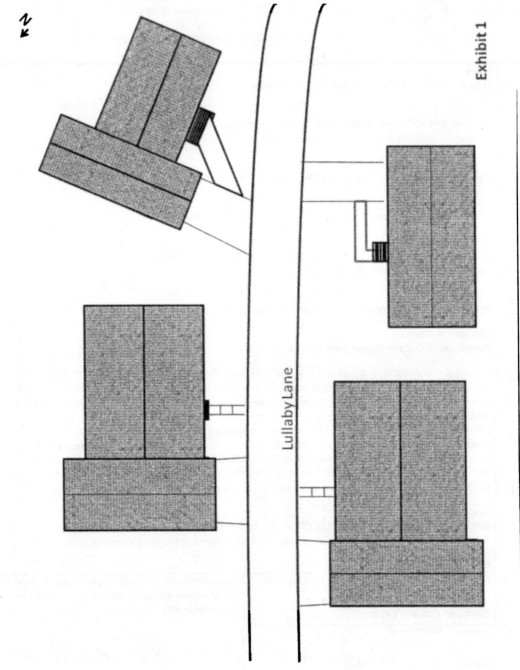

N

Lullaby Lane

Exhibit 1

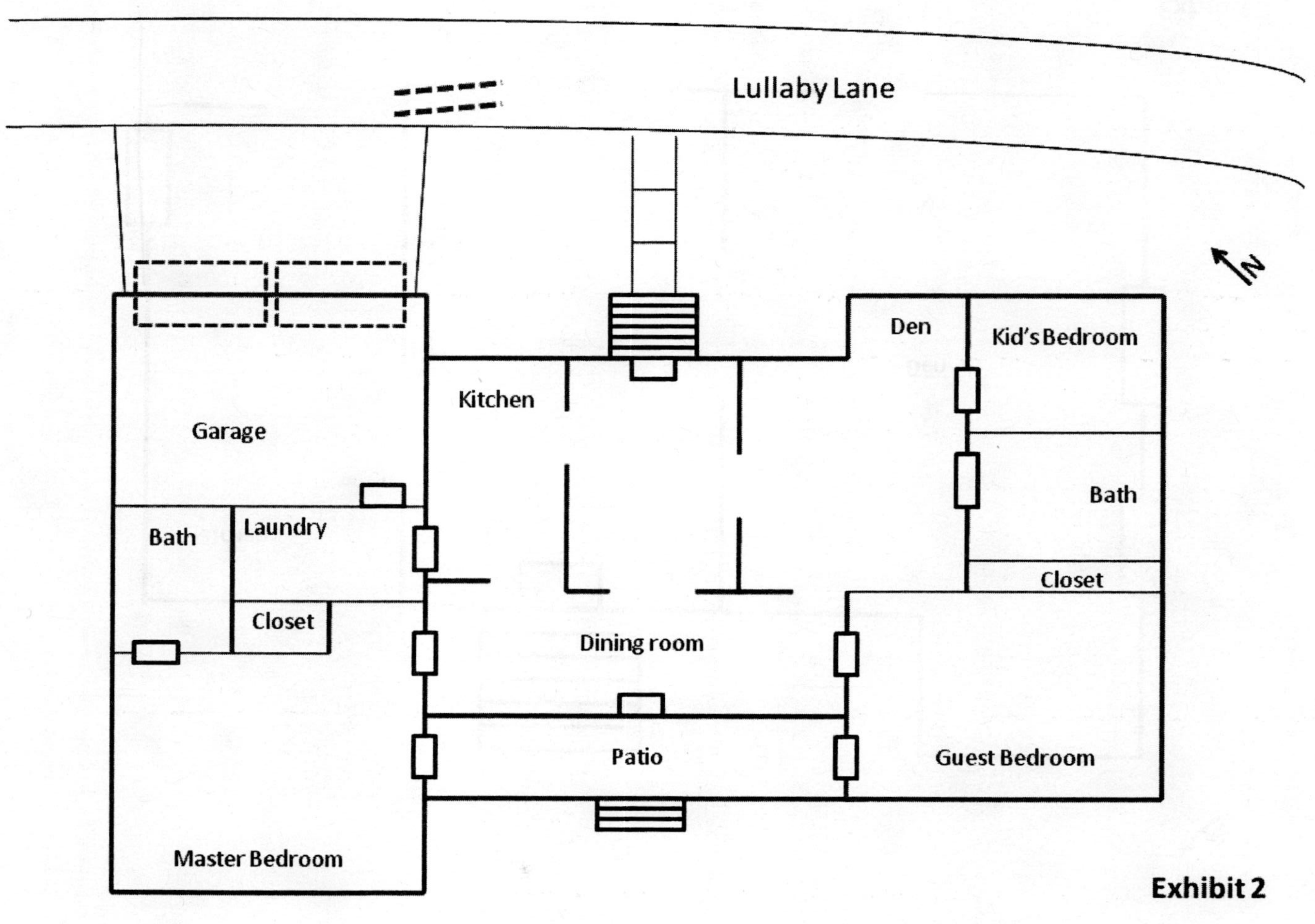
Lullaby Lane
N
Den
Kid's Bedroom
Kitchen
Garage
Bath
Bath
Laundry
Closet
Closet
Dining room
Patio
Guest Bedroom
Master Bedroom

Exhibit 2

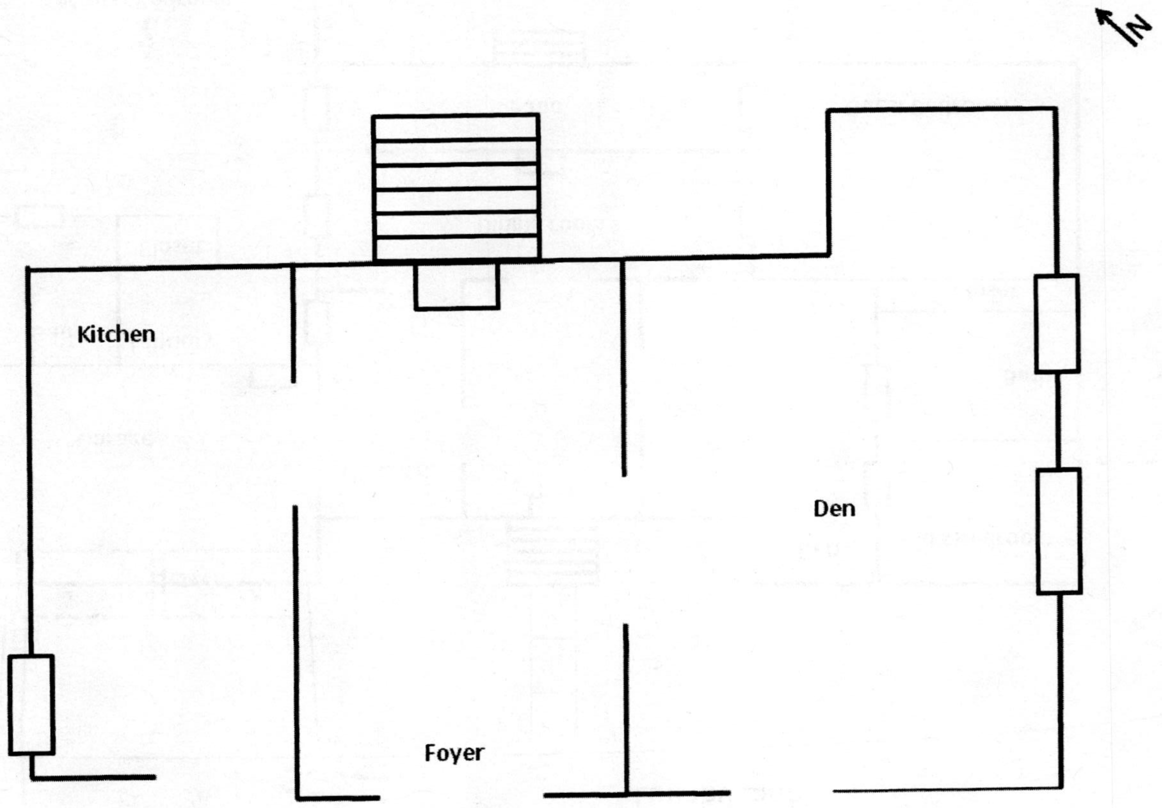

N

Kitchen

Den

Foyer

Exhibit 3

Hey Baby!

I was thinking of you tonight and my mind was wandering to when we will finally be together.

That wife of yours is such a bitch! I cannot wait to see her get hers. I will so make you happy. See you tonight!

NL
5/15/20XX-2
XXOOXXOO

Exhibit 4

Babe!

I wish I could see you some mo.

It has been too long since we been together. I'm startin' to think you might not be leaving her — better not be so.

I love you so much and I want us to have a baby together. Please kick that ho to the curb!

NL

6/1/20XX-2

Call ME or else....

Exhibit 5

Nikki's

where girls get their hair did ™

Can't wait to see you!

XXX OOO

Exhibit 6

Exhibit 7

Exhibit 8

Exhibit 9

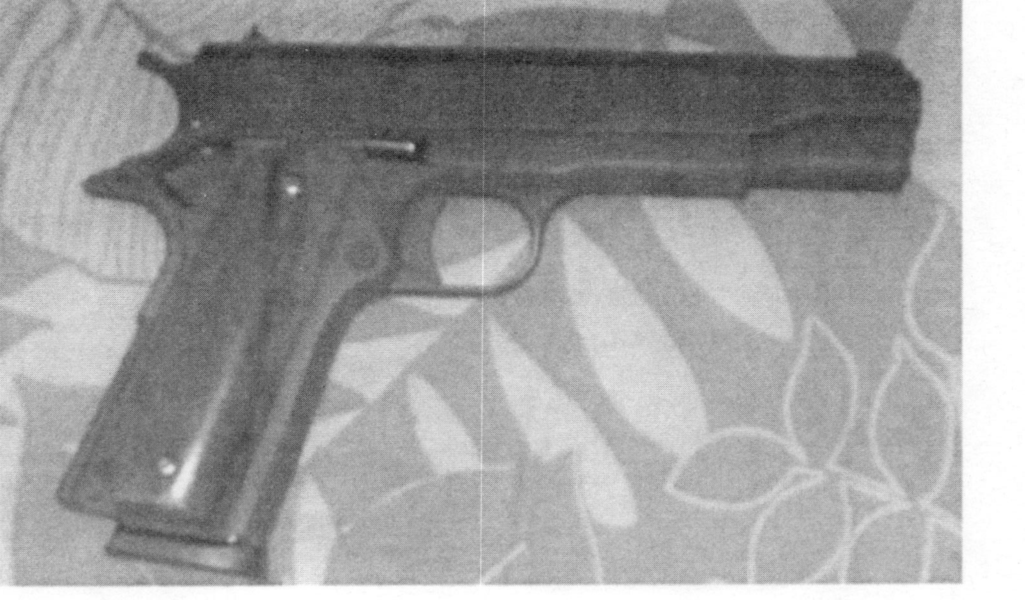

Exhibit 10

Exhibit 11

Exhibit 12

Exhibit 13

Exhibit 14

Exhibit 15

Exhibit 16

2 slugs retrieved from door jamb of Alexander home by ABW. Unable to conduct ballistics testing without a potential murder weapon.

Edwin Morris Jun 7, 20XX-2

Exhibit 17

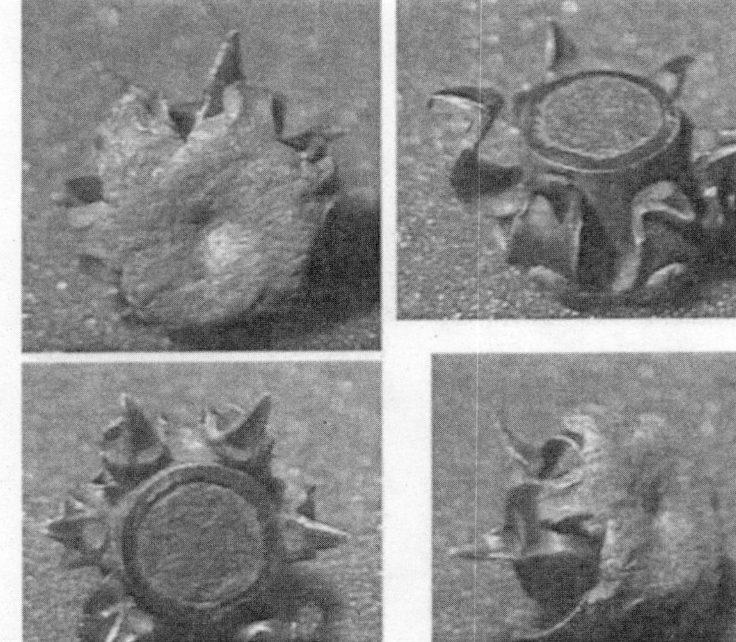

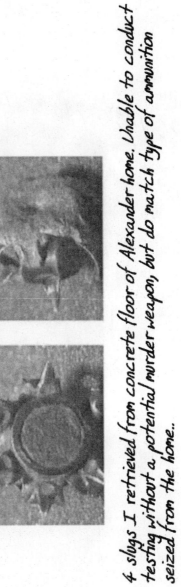

4 slugs I retrieved from concrete floor of Alexander home. Unable to conduct testing without a potential murder weapon, but do match type of ammunition seized from the home..

Edwin Morris Jun 7, 20XX-2

Exhibit 18

.45 caliber rounds retrieved by ABW from Alexander home on June 6, 20XX-2.

Edwin Morris Jun 7, 20XX-2

Exhibit 19

Exhibit 20

DE-1

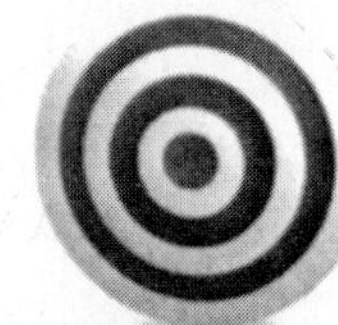

From My Cold Dead Hands

Pelican Bay Shooting Club

Sign In Roster

Name (Print & Sign)	Date/Time	Weapon	Range
Donald Sutherland	May 25, 20XX-2 0900 hours	9 MM Glock	2
Tyler Harder	May 25, 20XX-2 0945 hours	.22 caliber rifle	1
Wild Bill Ossmann	May 25, 20XX-2 10:13 AM	M1 Carbine	1
Brandi Alexander	May 25, 20XX-2	.45 Pistol	3
Chris Alexander	May 25, 20XX-2 11:25 AM	9 mm	4
Wild Bill Ossmann	May 25, 20XX-2 11:45 AM	.38	4
Norm Pearson	May 25, 20XX-2 1145 hours	.22 target pistol	3
Range closed for maintenance.	*1400 hours*	*B.B.S.*	

CALUSA POLICE DEPARTMENT
CALUSA COUNTY

INCIDENT REPORT
PAGE 1 OF 3

OFFICER'S NAME:	DATE:	TIME:	LOCATION:
Willie Alexander	1-6-200x-2	1442	West Calusa Hills

COMPLAINANT'S NAME:	DOB:	ADDRESS:	CITY / STATE ZIP
Robert Hightower		6732 Lullaby Lane	Pelican Bay, XX 33707

HOME PHONE NUMBER:	WORK PHONE NUMBER:	MOBILE/PAGER NUMBER:
727-555-3461	727-555-3465	n/a

ALLEGED SUSPECT'S NAME:	DOB:	ADDRESS:	CITY / STATE ZIP
Alias – Frosty	Unknown	Unknown	unknown

HOME PHONE NUMBER:	WORK PHONE NUMBER:	MOBILE/PAGER NUMBER:
n/a	n/a	n/a

(W1) WITNESS'S NAME:	DOB:	ADDRESS:	CITY / STATE ZIP
Juanita Hightower		6732 Lullaby Lane	Pelican Bay, XX 33707

HOME PHONE NUMBER:	WORK PHONE NUMBER:	MOBILE/PAGER NUMBER:

(W2) WITNESS'S NAME:	DOB:	ADDRESS:	CITY / STATE ZIP

HOME PHONE NUMBER:	WORK PHONE NUMBER:	MOBILE/PAGER NUMBER:

WRITE COMPLETE DETAILED REPORT:

Mr. Hightower called the Calusa County Sherrif's Department with a complaint that some unknown guy going by the name of frosty was selling drugs in the neighborhood. He complained that he watched the traffic in the neighborhood and he had noticed a lot of low rider type cars going by his house and parking on the street. Calusa County referred to PBPD. He also complained because he had called the Pelican Bay police department about gunfire in the neighborhood from some "hoodlums" down the street and nothing had been done. I canvassed the neighborhood but was unable to verify Mr. Hightower's allegations as to Frosty. Will refer to crime stoppers program for additional investigation.

OFFICER'S SIGNATURE	PRINTED NAME / RANK / BADGE NUMBER
Willie Alexander	Willie Hightower/SGT/7031D

Report Continued from Page 1:	

Mr. Hightower appeared combative and irritable when I told him I couldn't fine "Frosty." I smelled incense burning in the Hightower home, but did not observe any improper activity. I did find a group of gang members down the street that I ran off – they were just hanging Out and I observed no illegal activity.

---------------------------Nothing Follows-----------------------------------

OFFICER'S SIGNATURE	PRINTED NAME / RANK / BADGE NUMBER
Willie Alexander	Willie Alexander/SGT/7031D

INITIALS

WA

Report Continued from Page 2:	

------------------------------This Page Not Used------------------------------

OFFICER'S SIGNATURE	PRINTED NAME / RANK / BADGE NUMBER
Willie Alexander	Willie Alexander/SGT/7031D

REPORTING OFFICER	Willie Alexander		DATE REPORTED	1-6-200x-2
REPORTING OFFICER	Willie Alexander SIGNATURE		#7031D OFFICER BADGE	1-6-200x-2 DATE
REVIEWING SUPERVISOR	Willie Hightower SIGNATURE		#1240 OFFICER BADGE	1/6/200X-2 DATE

-Notes-

Bob's older brother is Eric w/the P.D.
commander of the PD
Assigned to investigate the death of Chris Alexander

Bob Hightower

Sworn Statement of Robert Hightower **July 4, 20XX-2**

RH page 1 of 2

My name is Bob Hightower. I am 44 years old. I was born and raised here in Pelican Bay. After high school, I went away to college at the University of Florida, where I received my B.S. in Physics and my Masters degree in Civil Engineering. After college, I decided to move back to Pelican Bay to get a job and start a family. Although I was offered a much higher-paying job in Biloxi, I just couldn't see myself living anywhere other than Pelican Bay. My entire family lives here and I love this city. I've been working at the same civil engineering firm for the past 15 years.

I have two older brothers. My oldest brother, Eric, is the commander of the Pelican Bay Police Department. He was actually the one assigned to investigate Chris Alexander's murder. Well, maybe not the murder itself, but I know he was the one who investigated the crime scene. I love Eric and would do anything for him. I think he is the best cop in the state. He would never lie for any reason and he always does his job perfectly.

My other brother is Ricky. He is the one we do not like to talk about much. You see, he never seemed to care about the consequences of his actions. He was in trouble with the law throughout high school and well into his adult life. Just a few years ago he finally got what was coming to him and was sentenced to twenty-five years for the attempted murder of his live-in girlfriend. He is still in jail and that is where he deserves to stay. He has been nothing but a disgrace to our entire family.

One of the main reasons I don't like Ricky is because he got me caught up in some of his criminal problems a few years back. He approached me around ten years ago to drive him around for work and such because his car broke down. I decided to help him because he had some recent problems with the law and I wanted to help him get his life back in order. Anyway, after I picked him up one day from a friend's house, a police officer pulled me over because I had a broken taillight. My brother told me just to "play it cool." I had no idea what he was talking about. The cop noticed that something was off and asked both of us to step out of the car. They ultimately found marijuana on him and a small bag underneath the seat. Because they were charging me with felony possession, I accepted the prosecutor's plea deal and testified against Ricky. Because I testified, they only gave me six months probation. conviction B.S.

The only other legal trouble I had was with the IRS back in the early '90s. It happened because I forgot to include $10,000 worth of investment income on my tax return. The IRS brought charges of fraud and tax evasion against me. However, they eventually dropped the charges because I was very compliant and quickly paid all the taxes, plus penalties, and interest. charges dropped

Although I have lived across the street from the Alexanders for several years, I really didn't talk much to either Brandi or Chris. Chris knew my brother, Ricky. So, I guess the adage is true—you know—the company you keep and all. Anyway, I didn't know Brandi or Chris, really. However, I do know a little bit about each of their reputations around town.

With Brandi, I think it is common knowledge that Brandi knew her husband was cheating on her with at least two women. She had the reputation as being a woman who was reaching her breaking point. One of my friends saw her at the grocery store the day of the murder and told me that she looked angry and ready to pop. I just think she could not tolerate the cheating and lies anymore. Brandi also had a reputation of being a hothead. I had a dispute with her about her children hitting a baseball through my window and she just would not listen to me. I tried to talk to her calmly and explain to her that I only wanted her to pay for the window. Instead of talking, she screamed and yelled at me. She told me not to lecture her on how to raise her children. I think that is exactly what happened when she shot Chris. My guess is that she just would not listen to her husband's excuses and snapped.

I think it is common knowledge that Chris had issues with drugs, but nothing serious, just marijuana. I have seen some very disreputable people come by his house a few times when I was up late reading on my porch, especially in the last year or so. They would go in his house for only one or two minutes and then leave holding something in their hands. Everyone knew he liked to buy and sell small amounts of marijuana. I don't know if it means anything, but I found a very odd note in my car one day that stated, "Hey, if you need more to sell, let me know. C.A." I am positive the note fell out of Ricky's pocket because I just dropped him off at work, and it wasn't in my car when I picked him up. Also, although I don't know for sure, I think it was Chris Alexander's handwriting on the note.

On the night of Chris's murder, I was sound asleep in my bedroom when I heard what sounded like gunfire. It was so loud that I thought it was coming from my front yard. Concerned for my family's safety, I grabbed my .45 caliber gun and ran towards the window to see what was going on. I looked out the front window and didn't see anything in my yard or the Alexanders' yard across the street. I didn't hear anyone's house alarm going off. I certainly didn't see any car speeding away. The cops, including my brother Eric, came to my house to ask me questions about forty-five minutes after I heard the shots. I was completely truthful to them and told them everything I knew. I made sure to tell them about Chris and Brandi's reputations. In the end, I am positive that Brandi shot Chris. I just have this feeling about it that will not go away. I am normally never wrong about these things.

RH page 2 of 2

Signed: Robert Hightower

July 4, 20XX-2

Witnessed by: Detective Edwin Morris

Signed, Edwin Morris

July 8, 20XX-2

Sworn Statement of Nikki Long **July 8, 20XX-2**

NL page 1 of 2

My name is Nikki Long. I hereby swear under penalty of perjury that the following is a true and accurate recounting of all relevant events that I can remember concerning my relationship with Chris Alexander and the time leading up to his death. I believe this statement to be a true and complete version of events as I remember them. I told my story to Detective Morris who then typed it up and let me review it.

My name is Nikki Long. I'm 25 years old. I own Nikki's Beauty Shop. I have been working there since I was 19. I actually met Chris, two years ago, while I was at the Salon. The day I met Chris is a day I will never forget. It was love at first sight. I was outside of the salon taking my 15 minute break, when all the sudden this fine, dark, tall, handsome man pulled up in the parking lot. He was on his way to Pro Style. Pro Style is a barber shop for men that's next door to Nikki's. When he walked by me he asked me for the time, and since I knew I had to make an impression I told him it was time for him to meet the girl of his dreams. Of course he laughed, and he actually missed that appointment he had for his hair cut. We sat outside and talked for about 2 hours. After that day Chris and I were in separable. Well almost, the only time we spent apart was when he had to go home to Brandi and the kids.

Brandi was jealous of me. Jealous that I'm younger, jealous that I'm prettier and thinner, jealous that her man loved and wanted me. It started to go downhill really bad with Chris and Brandi when she found out I was pregnant. When I found out I was going to have Chris's baby I couldn't keep it a secret. I told everyone at the salon that they were going to have to start planning my baby shower because I was about to be a mommy! I knew Brandi was going to find out about the baby because she was friends with people who came to Nikki's, and she got her hair done there a few times as well.

I ended up losing that baby and when that happened I didn't go to work for, like, 3 weeks. I was miserable, I was sad because Chris and I were finally going to have a child, we were going to be a family and I lost all that when I lost the baby. I didn't know if he would leave "her" once I lost the baby and worrying about that nearly broke my heart. When I finally decided to come back to work, Brandi was there getting her hair done. When she saw me, she said "sorry to hear about your loss, but good things never happen to bad people." I couldn't believe she said that to me. If I didn't love Chris so much, and have so much respect for his family, I would have slapped her right then and there. I did swear at her, calling her a bad word and promised her that she would "get" hers someday.

very NL

Chris's family is^important in our town. His family is respected, and I would never want to do anything that would cause drama for them so I calmed down after I yelled at her. I just smirked at her and went to my station to get ready for the day. I felt like I shouldn't waste any more breath on Brandi, I had what she wanted. I had her man

And I was keeping him too!

NL

I told Chris about what Brandi said to me at my job, and he assured me not to worry about her. He said that Brandi did this to herself. He told me that Brandi did not have feelings for him anymore, and all she cared about was her own self-image. They weren't even sleeping in the same room. He would sleep on the couch, and the only reason he had not left her was because of the kids. And he promised me that it wouldn't be long until he left her for good and would marry me.

Chris and I were going to get married, and Brandi knew it. That's why she did what she did. On the night of Chris's murder, Chris went out with his brother. I was going to go out with them that evening, but I had 3 perms, and 2 press and curls that day and I was exhausted. I told Chris, to just call me on his way home so I knew he made it home safe. Chris always called to kiss me goodnight, so I waited by the phone. Chris called me while he was on his way home. He told me that he had stopped at Wendy's for a burger. Chris always got a burger and a drink before he went home. He seemed to have a lot of friends at the Wendy's. He told me that you should never go to sleep on an empty stomach, especially after drinking.

While we were on the phone, Chris told me that he wanted us to move in together. He said that he and Brandi got into an argument earlier that day, and he told her it was over. He said that he told her he would be leaving by the end of the week. I was so excited that Chris was finally leaving Brandi. I had been sharing Chris for two years, and finally he would be all mine. My conversation with Chris lasted around 35 minutes. I heard him use his keys to open the door, and I heard him reset the alarm to his house. I also heard him turn on the TV, and then he complained that his order was wrong. They put onions on his burger, and Chris hates onions. All of a sudden Chris then said "I'll call you back". I asked him is she in front of you, and he said yes. Whenever Chris would say I'll call you back, especially when he says it suddenly, then, that's my signal to just hang up, and I know he will call me back when Brandi leaves the room.

My Chris did not call me back that night. I never got my goodnight kiss from him. I learned that two minutes after we hung up he was killed. I guess she figured if she couldn't have him, then neither could I.

NL page 2 of 2

Nikki Long

Nikki Long
July 8, 200x-2

Witnessed by: Detective Edwin Morris

Signed, *Edwin Morris*

July 8, 200x-2

Sworn Statement of Sharon Barry **August 12, 20XX-1**

S.B page 1 of 2

My name is Sharon Barry. I hereby swear under penalty of perjury that the following is a true and accurate recounting of all relevant events that I can remember concerning my interactions with Brandi and Chris Alexander.

I first met the defendant, Brandi Alexander about six months before Chris Alexander passed away. According to the insurance policy the date that we met was January 5, 20XX-2.

At the time I worked for Friends Helping Friends (FHF) Insurance as an insurance agent. Currently, I am no longer employed with FHF Insurance. I work for another insurance company, as a supervising agent.

According to my notes, I was contacted by Chris Alexander in mid-December of 20XX-3 to meet with him and his wife. They were looking to purchase an insurance policy for Chris Alexander in the event that he passed away, so that he could make sure that his wife and children were taken care of financially. I specifically remember that it was Chris who called because I thought it was such a responsible thing for a husband and father to do.

The meeting on January 5, 20XX-2 took place at the Alexander' home. The meeting took place at 6 pm after both Brandi and Chris were home from work. The meeting was routine. I received personal information from both Brandi and Chris regarding their ages, health, family history, and other insurance policies or health coverage. At that time, I was made aware that Chris had another insurance policy, which was issued by Chris's employer for roughly $80,000. We talked about all of their options, and I remember filling out a worksheet with them establishing that Chris was underinsured – not uncommon for folks his age by the way.

After completing all the relevant insurance forms, Brandi and Chris obtained coverage for Chris at $250,000. This insurance amount was based on the monthly cost of the policy. A higher insurance amount would have cost them more money each month, and they were unable to afford any higher coverage. The premium is based on all the personal information that was provided to me at the time. The premium amounts are pre-set based on the personal information. I followed the proper procedures outlined by FHF Insurance when providing the coverage amount and monthly cost.

At that time Brandi declined to insure herself. It was my understanding that Brandi and Chris made this decision after talking over the monthly cost of life insurance for either both of them, or just for one. I am unaware how or why this decision was reached. After providing them with an insurance quote, I allowed Brandi and Chris to talk about their decision in private. I went outside while they were talking in private, and they called me back into the house when they had made a decision. Chris signed the paperwork that day.

Chris listed Brandi, his wife, as his sole beneficiary.

I had no further contact with either Brandi or Chris until after Chris was killed. About 4 days after Chris died, Brandi called me. Brandi told me that Chris was murdered and that she needed to claim his life insurance. She qualified her desire for the life insurance collection in such a short period of time after his death, because she needed the money to help cover funeral expenses. This was not unusual, since funeral homes expect payment when services are rendered.

I immediately put the claim through to my superiors at FHF Insurance, and a check was ready within a few days. I called Brandi back that same day and told her that the claim was processing. We talked a long time. Brandi seemed so terribly distraught and in need of sympathy and attention. I asked Brandi if it was okay for me to come by and pay my respects. She told me where she was staying, since Chris died in her home, she said she was staying at her mother's house. Brandi told me she could not bear to go back into her house, the place where the love of her life was brutally murdered.

I took the next few days off of work and stayed by Brandi's side, along with her other friends and family. We became instantly close, and, as sad as this is, we bonded during her time of mourning. To this day we remain friends. We talk on the phone at least twice a week; we go to dinner and movies together.

I enjoy Brandi's company. She is such an honest, sweet, and caring person. It was devastating when she was charged with Chris's murder. There is no way she could have killed Chris. She only spoke fondly of him, regardless of his affairs. She knew that Chris loved her more than any other woman. She told me over and over again how she refused to leave her. Brandi is a wonderful mother too. Her children are well-behaved, polite and adorable. This is because Brandi has raised them properly, like a good-hearted woman would.

S.B page 2 of 2

Sharon Barry

Sharon Barry
August 12, 20XX-1

Witnessed by: Detective Edwin Morris

Signed, Edwin Morris

August 12, 20XX-1

* Next Door Neighbor

Witness Name: *Doris Presley*
Date Statement taken: *August 12, 20xx-2*
Investigator: *Dana Stubbs*

I remember the night Chris Alexander was killed. I don't remember the exact date, but I clearly remember what happened that night.. How could I forget? I've been Mr. and Mrs. Alexander' neighbor for about fifteen years. They were always such a nice couple. We would say hello in passing and Mr. Alexander sometimes mowed my lawn for me. Their children were always so polite. They where such a nice family... That's why it was such a shock to me when he was killed.

On the night Mr. Alexander was murdered I was on the phone with my aunt. My mom's 65th birthday was that coming weekend and my aunt and I were talking about the surprise party we were planning on throwing for her. Aunt Nancy is a bit old and hard of hearing so we were talking pretty loud. No matter though, I sure heard those gunshots. They were very loud. Scared me half to death they did. At first I didn't know what it was exactly. I thought it might have been a car backfiring, but they came so close together I knew it couldn't be that. It's just so unusual to hear gun shots in my neighborhood I didn't know what to do. That neighbor Mr. Hightower has fired his pistol in the neighborhood a time or two and it sounded a lot like that.

Next thing I know, I heard a car screeching out of the driveway next door. I was too afraid to go to the window and look, but I heard the car pull out of the driveway and head east away from my home. I would say the screeching happened only seconds later – it all happened so fast. I didn't go outside because I don't like to go out after dark. The cops never came by to talk with me about it and I thought they knew about the car. I called the DA's office to offer my help but they never came by either. As God is my witness this is my memory of the events that evening.

Signed: Doris Presley

Witness Name: *Billy Bob Schifflett*
Date Statement taken: *August 14, 20xx-2*
Investigator: *Dana Stubbs*

My name is Billy Bob Schifflett and I own the "From My Cold Dead Hands" Shootin' club in Pelican Bay. Well, actually we sit outside the city limits in Calusa County. We are really part of Gulfport, a small unincorporated place where folks can do what they like without the government interfering in our business. Gulfport has a long history of folks that like on the outskirts of society and we like it that way – for good reason.

I've owned the club for about 5 years now, I won it in a poker game from a fellow that ain't around here no more. I pay my taxes, high though they are, and I don't cause nobody no trouble and I intends to keep it that way.

I don't remember who actually came into the Shooting club to use the range on the 25th of May, 20XX-2, but we do have specific procedures that the federal government requires us to follow and I've been following them since 911.

Whenever anyone comes in I make them take a short safety test, we give them a briefing and then check their ID to make certain that they are who they claim to be. They go downstairs to the shooting range to use it. We don't go downstairs with them, but we do control access to the

Witness Name: *Billy Bob Schifflett*
Date Statement taken: *August 14, 20xx-2*
Investigator: *Dana Stubbs*

shooting range area. All of our ranges, and we got 4 of them, are downstairs. Range 1 is a rifle range and the other three are for pistols. They are underground for safety reasons.

Once shooters get downstairs they have to sign in on our sign in sheet. I don't watch them do that, and they are on their own honor to do it. Gun owners are usually sticklers for following rules – it's a safety thing.

I know both Chris and Brandi Alexander. I went to school with them and Chris has bought quite a few guns from me over the years. He's bought pistols and rifles. I sold him a .45 caliber pistol about a year ago that was Army surplus. Brandi's come here with him once or twice, but I don't specifically remember seeing her anytime in the club in the last 6 months.

I have provided you guys with a copy of our sign in roster like you asked. I did close the range around 2 on the 25th of May 20XX-2. I waited till no one was using it. I don't remember how much brass we cleaned up that day and what type of guns were fired. You'd have to check the roster and talk to the folks on it.

Signed: Billy Bob Schifflett

NL page 1 of 1

My name is Nikki Long. I have thought a long time about what happened that awful night and I have more information that I need to tell you. I've been racking my brains trying to remember exactly what it was I heard and last night in a dream it came to me.

When Chris said "I'll call you back" I got angry at him. I'm ashamed to admit it but I had really been pissed at him for not leaving Brandi yet and I yelled at him. Yes, I know, I'm so ashamed to admit it but I yelled at my darling Chris in those last moments before he died. He started to say something and then I heard Brandi through the phone. She was yelling. I heard her say "Are you talking to that whore Nikki Long? I told you to stay away from that slut!"

Then I heard a door slam. Chris said to me "look baby I gotta...." And then all of a sudden I heard these loud banging sounds. Right after that I heard a gun go off several times and then I heard someone pick up the cell phone and the line went dead.

I hope she burns in Hell for taking Chris away from me that night.

NL page 2 of 2

Nikki Long

Nikki Long
July 19, 20xx-1

Witnessed by: Detective Edwin Morris

Signed, Edwin Morris

July 19, 20XX-1

Affidavit - Officer Anece Baxter-White **July 13, 20XX-1**

My name is Anece Baxter-White. I hereby swear under penalty of perjury that the following is a true and accurate recounting of all relevant events related to my involvement in this case. I have prepared this affidavit at the request of the prosecuting attorney in the case of *State v. Alexander*. I was the officer on the scene the night of Chris Alexander's murder. I have been a police officer for Calusa County for the past 15 years. During this time, I have investigated about 50 shootings, as well as numerous other violent crimes. I have been trained in the collection of evidence by the Calusa County Police Department.

On the night of June 3, 20XX-2, our department received a 911 call at 11:16 pm from the defendant's PDQ alarm service reporting a shooting. Myself and other officers were sent to the scene by our dispatch office. To my knowledge we did not receive a 911 call from the defendant herself. I arrived at the scene at some point after the call. I wrote in my report that I arrived at 11:01pm, but I know that this is incorrect, because we didn't receive the 911 call until 11:16pm. I was about 10 minutes away from the neighborhood when I received the call.

Outside of the home, I observed skid marks on the road in front of the defendant's driveway. The front of the home had nice landscaping, with several trees and rose bushes. It seemed like a nice upper-middle class neighborhood. A few neighbors were standing on their front lawns observing the situation. I directed another officer to interview some of the neighbors to search for leads. The defendant's front windows were closed, but the front drapes were open. When I approached the front door, I noticed several shell casings on the ground and heard the defendant crying. She appeared to be in distress; she was in the living room kneeling beside her husband's body, shaking him, and yelling at him to wake up. The paramedics had to pull her away from the body.

The body was located in the living room. The deceased was lying on his back, but it was unclear whether he had been standing or sitting when he was shot. Further inspection of the body revealed that the decedent had sustained multiple gun wounds, including two (2) shots to the groin area, which usually indicates a crime of passion. There were also two (2) bullets found in the concrete underneath the body, which could indicate that the gun was fired after the decedent had already fallen. The only blood present at the scene was that underneath the decedent, which lead me to believe he was not moved after death, and was shot and killed in the room he was found in. The bullets came from a .45 caliber gun. We turned the bullets over to ballistics for testing.

Besides the bullets in the body, I also observed a bullet lodged in the doorway to the foyer. The positioning of the bullet indicated that the shooter was probably standing near the front door when they fired the gun. There were multiple bullet holes in the home. We retrieved several slugs, but the rounds fired were hollow points that broke apart on impact. I also discovered bullets in the interior walls of the living room and the foyer inside the home. No viable samples for ballistics testing could be located and I cannot state with any degree of certainty the weapon that fired these rounds.

ABW Page 2 of 2

Upon further investigation of the house, I noticed the decedent's shirt and shoes in the living room. The television was turned on, and there was a bag of Wendy's food on the table. There was a small bag of marijuana and another of cocaine inside the takeout bag. It appeared that the decedent had been watching TV in the living room, was drawn to the foyer for some reason, then was shot. I also walked through out the house prior to speaking with Ms. Alexander. I looked at all of the windows and none appeared to have been broken or tampered with. I noted that the alarm system was activated and currently functioning. I then attempted to talk to Ms. Alexander but she was incredibly upset, weeping, screaming, almost howling.

When the defendant finally calmed down, I asked her what had happened. She told me she was asleep in her bed, and was awaken by a sound which she thought was her air conditioning. She smelt smoke and got up to investigate. She then observed the front door open, and saw her husband lying on the ground. She determined he was dead. She stated her PDQ alarm company called her, and they called 911 for her. I then asked her if she had a gun. She replied that she did not. However, when I searched the defendant's bedroom, I found an empty gun holster, belonging to a 9 mm gun, underneath the bed. I asked her again if she had a gun. This time she replied she did, and led me to a 9mm gun she kept high on a shelf in the laundry room. This gun used to shoot the decedent, a .45 caliber revolver, was not recovered.

Gun in the home?

The defendant's children were also home. They slept through the shooting, and did not wake up when myself and the detectives arrived. I found this to be unusual, because gun shots are loud, and the children's bedroom was in very close proximity to the living room. However, there was no evidence found at the scene to indicate that the children had been drugged. There did appear to be 8 empty Benadryl cellophane packets on the kitchen table but Ms. Alexander stated, and the parents of Chris Alexander verified, that the children had been sick with colds.

After about 3 hours of searching the home and interviewing the defendant, my team and I left. Once I got back to the station it was determined that a GSR test of the defendant's hands would be necessary. The test was conducted after the time we had left the home. We did not maintain constant supervision with the defendant between the time we left the scene and when the GSR test was conducted.

Anece Baxter-White

Anece Baxter-White
July 13, 20XX-1

Gun shot Residue test

IN THE CIRCUIT COURT OF THE FIRST JUDICIAL DISTRICT
CALUSA COUNTY
CRIMINAL DIVISION

State

v.

Brandi Alexander

CASE NO.: 0318-20XX

DEPOSITION OF: Roger Curlin

TAKEN BY: State

BEFORE: COURT REPORTER Vilma Rodriquez
PELICAN BAY COURT REPORTERS
2113 Veritas Way
PELICAN BAY, XX 33707

DATE: September 11, 20XX-2

LOCATION: Criminal Justice Center
6745 49th Avenue South
Pelican Bay, XX 33707

State Attorney Questioning Begins:

Q: Please state your name and Profession.
A: My name is Roger Curlin and I am a Forensic Scientist with the State Bureau of Investigation. I have held that position for the last fifteen years.
Q: What is your educational background?
A: I graduated from University of Phoenix with a Bachelor of Science in Biochemistry and received my Masters degree from the University of Phoenix.

Q: Do you have a doctorate?
A: No, I was working on my doctorate when I had some family issues, so I have not completed my dissertation in order to obtain my doctorate degree. I have done all the course work.
Q: What types of forensic science do you specialize in?
A: I do not specialize in any type of forensic science because I find that too restricting, instead I am broadly trained and skilled in a variety of forensic specialties.
Q: What investigative steps did you take involving the Alexander murder?
A: On June 3, 200x-2, I was summoned by the Pelican Bay Police Department to the home of Chris and Brandi Alexander. I conducted an initial examination of the crime scene and determined that the shooter in this case should have gunshot residue on their person and hands.
Q: What is a gunshot residue test?
A: A GSR test is the most common test performed to determine if a person was in the presence of gunshot residue within a limited time period after a weapon is discharged.
Q: How do you test for gunshot residue?
A: The test is pretty simple and the procedure is performed all over the United States and is admitted as evidence in many criminal cases. Like I said, the test is fairly simple. When someone fires a gun, the gun releases a

pattern of particles that leave a residue. This residue is comprised of a combination of lead, barium, and antimony particles that are fused together. The same explosion that forces the bullet out of the gun also releases these particles into an invisible cloud that leaves traces of residue on the shooter's hand, surrounding area, and the victim's body. In order to determine if a person has fired a gun, the procedure is to swab the area of the suspect's hand to collect any residue present. Then, we analyze the swabs with a GSR machine that determines if the swab samples are positive for traces of GSR and, if so, to what extent.

Q: When do you test someone for GSR?

A: I test the individual or individuals the detective on the scene wishes to have tested. In this case, that would be the defendant, Brandi Alexander.

Q: Where was this test conducted?

A: At the Alexanders' residence. I tested Mrs. Alexander at her home. I swabbed both hands and placed the cotton swabs into two sterile bags; one for the left hand and one for the right hand. I noted that Mrs. Alexander's dominant hand was her right. I later performed the analysis, and I determined that there was at least one particle of GSR from the left hand swab taken from Mrs. Alexander.

Q: What do you need to ensure the most accurate results?

A: For the most accurate results, a GSR sample should be taken within five (5) hours of the initial gunshot. I performed the test on Mrs. Alexander within three (3) hours of the shooting, but if Mrs. Alexander washed her hands or had substantial contact with anything, the amount of GSR on her hands at the time of the swab would be reduced.

Q: Does the fact that you are not specifically trained in GSR testing affect the validity of your test results?

A: No. Although I do not have extensive expertise or education in the analysis or methodology of GSR, I did take the course that was offered by the manufacturer of the GSR machine we use to analyze the swabs. I do not think there is a need for any additional training, in fact, there is not really that much to know. Either there is GSR on the suspect or there is not, it is as simple as that. In my mind, if there is GSR present then the person must have fired a weapon recently. I am not aware of any studies that have dealt with other ways in which GSR might contaminate a scene, and I have not studied the predicted GSR patterns for types of weapons.

Q: You are qualified to conduct the test and record results?

A: Yes, that is a fair and accurate description of what I do.

Q: I have no further questions.

//Defense Counsel declined to question the witness during the deposition//

Medical Examiner

IN THE CIRCUIT COURT OF THE FIRST JUDICIAL DISTRICT
CALUSA COUNTY
CRIMINAL DIVISION

State v. Brandi Alexander	CASE NO.: 0318-20XX

DEPOSITION OF: Dr. Jeremiah Jones

TAKEN BY: State

BEFORE: COURT REPORTER Vilma Rodriquez
PELICAN BAY COURT REPORTERS
2113 Veritas Way
PELICAN BAY, XX 33707

DATE: September 12, 20XX-2

LOCATION: Criminal Justice Center
6745 49th Avenue South
Pelican Bay, XX 33707

State Attorney Questioning Begins:

Q: Please state your name and Profession.

A: My name is Dr. Jeremiah Jones, and I am both the County Coroner and Medical Examiner for Calusa County. I have held that position for the last twenty years.

Q: What is your educational background?

A: I graduated from State University with a Bachelor of Science in chemistry and attended medical school in Grenada. I completed my residency in 20XX-24. For the

first four years I worked in the emergency room of Calusa County Hospital and then became the county coroner in 20XX-20.
Q: Do you have any specializations?
A: Yes. I have conducted advanced studies in medical examiner training. I have also been on Court TV many times. They affectionately refer to me as Dr. Death on that show. I try to share my years of expertise with the audience.
Q: What types of forensic science do you specialize in?
A: I specialize in cause of death investigations. I am particularly adept at event reconstruction as determined by the placement, angle, velocity and burn mark patterns associated with gunshot wounds.
Q: What investigative steps did you take involving the Alexander murder?
A: I conducted the initial examination to determine the cause of death.
Q: How did you accomplish this?
A: I conducted an initial examination of Mr. Alexander's body when it was first brought into the county morgue. It was immediately obvious that he died from gunshot wounds to both the groin and chest. I determined that the manner of death was homicide and that the cause of death was by gunshot.
Q: What happened after you conducted this initial examination?

A: I put on my M.E. hat and got down to work. I performed an autopsy of Mr. Alexander in order to determine why he died.
Q: What did you determine?
A: I determined that Mr. Alexander was shot twice in the chest of 4 times in the groin. Based upon the pattern of blood splatter it was evident that the groin injuries occurred first.
Q: Is it really possible to determine that?
A: Absolutely. The flow of blood internally, when combined with the information provided by the investigating police officers made it clear. I don't even need to see any alleged blood splatter patterns to make this determination. The wounds in the body are the controlling factor when analyzing cause of death here.
Q: Which shots caused the death of Mr. Alexander?
A: Clearly the groin shots. It appears that he was shot in the groin, severing at least one femoral artery. He was then allowed to bleed for approximately 10 minutes, probably while being held at gunpoint. Once he had "bled out" a great deal the coup de grace was administered by shooting him twice in the chest.
Q: Doctor, to what degree of medical certainty can you state this opinion as to the cause of death?
A: I am completely certain of it. I would stake my reputation on it.

Q: I have no further Questions.

//Defense Counsel declined to question the witness during the deposition//

Excerpts from Prior Sworn Testimony of Brandi Alexander
1st Criminal Trial

DIRECT EXAMINATION

Defense Counsel Begins

Q: Mrs. Alexander, please introduce yourself to the jury.
A: My name is Brandi Alexander, and I am the defendant in this case.
Q: Tell us about yourself.
A: I am the youngest of three children. My parents always jokingly referred to me as their "little Einstein." I was really bookish and nerdy as a kid. Unlike most teens, I didn't really rebel, do drugs, or get into alcohol. I liked school and put my energies into doing well. My brother and sister always gave me a hard time about it. They used to joke that I was "old before my time."
Q: When did you first meet your husband?
A: I first met Chris in high school in 20XX-14. He was a year behind me in school.
Q: What do you remember about him then?
A: I remember he was popular, athletic, and liked girls and cars. Girls liked him, too, but the rumor was that he liked to love girls and then leave them. So, of course, I was a little worried when he started to date one of my girlfriends, Cynthia. They dated only for a short while during my senior year.

Q: What interaction did you have with him back then?
A: Chris and Cynthia had gone together to the senior prom. I remember that night pretty well, partially because my date had broken his leg that very same day and couldn't make it, and partly because Cynthia was angry with Chris because he wanted to stop by Wendy's before the dance. I laughed when she told me the story and she stormed off saying that I was naive and "didn't know anything" leaving Chris and me alone at the punch bowl.
Q: What happened then?
A: Chris seemed embarrassed and made some small talk. When he learned I didn't have a date for the evening, he didn't make me feel bad about not having a date and went out of his way to include me without hurting Cynthia's feelings. He was very nice to me. I remember thinking he was handsome, smart, and funny. He had a nice smile. Cynthia and I made up later that night. The three of us had a great time at the prom.
Q: When was the next time you got together with Chris?
A: Oh it was years later. Chris and I met again --oh, I think it was in May of 20XX-11. It was right before my college graduation. I had just had my hair done at the hair salon when I ran into him. He recognized me first. He told me he was going in to the barber shop next door to get a shave and a haircut. Other than a well-kept a goatee, Chris looked the same as he did in high school—he had that same easy smile.

Q: What did you two talk about?
A: We made some small talk and laughed about prom night. I told Chris that Cynthia had died last year from breast cancer. Chris said he knew her husband well and that he had visited Cynthia at home a few times before she had passed. We discussed how Cynthia had turned to medical use of marijuana to ease her pain, even though it had not been prescribed for her. Chris said he heard that too, and agreed that Cynthia's last weeks had been sad and tragic.
Q: Did you see him again?
A: Yes. When Chris suggested we have lunch together sometime, I mentioned there wasn't a Wendy's for several miles and said I didn't like their Frosties. Chris laughed. He said he loved Wendy's and would forgive me that. He also joked that he understood now that Wendy's was off-limits for a "first date"—he learned that much from prom night. Then he asked for my number and promised to call me, which he did later that night. We made a date for the following weekend and dated for several months afterward.
Q: Were you working then?
A: No, but shortly thereafter I got a job as an elementary school teacher after graduation. I taught third grade at Pelican Bay Elementary School, only four blocks from my parents' home.
Q: Did Chris work?

A: Unlike me, Chris never went to college after high school. He always told me that college wasn't his "thing." Although most of his family was in law enforcement or civil service, Chris always told me that he preferred to work with his hands and he couldn't stand the idea of being in a job where people told him what to do just because they outranked him. He said he "gave up the chance to join the Army" for that very reason and went to trade school instead. After graduating from trade school, Chris had landed a good job as a tool and die maker for Industrial Metal Fabrication (IMF) Company, less than a mile from my parents' home. He said the flexible swing-shift hours, high hourly pay, union protection, and benefits suited him well.

Q: Did your husband have a lot of contacts in the community?

A: While we were dating, Chris always ran into people he knew. Although they were friendly with Chris, none of them really seemed to know him that well. The women we ran into made me nervous—they were very forward with Chris and touched him a lot, which was not my style. Chris would tell me not to mind the other girls—that I was the one for him. He said he liked that I was "old fashioned" and looked out for him, and he never let anyone, man or woman, get too close. He said that friends were less important to him than family, and I was family. I liked that he worried about what I thought. His popularity made me feel important and proud of him.

Q: What did your family think of him?
A: My family liked Chris well enough. My mom never seemed to warm up to him, though. I just figured it was my mom being a mom—she was always protective of me and my siblings. My brother and sister lived in town, but met Chris only two times before Chris and I were married. They all got along fine. Chris and I were married on December 20, 200x-10. Chris and I never had sex before marriage—mostly because we agreed it should be that way. Chris respected who I was and I never felt otherwise.
Q: How did you get along with his family?
A: Good most of the time. Chris had a large extended family—blood relatives, distant cousins, and friends of the family made up the majority of his social network. They were very different from my own family in that they distrusted outsiders and seemed "larger than life."
Q: How did you adjust to his family?
A: Well, you know ,Chris was different around them. He talked loudly and irreverently. Chris was always the center of attention and seemed to lose himself in the attention they lavished on him. They called Chris often—at home, on his cell. There seemed to be no boundaries among them, except one: Chris always insisted that people call him before they dropped by the house. This was Chris's golden rule, and no

one ever violated it. They usually called Chris on his cell, but it was not unusual for people to call the house as well.

Q: Was there anything else about Chris's behavior that seemed strange to you?

A: It was not unusual for Chris to head out in the middle of the night to have drinks, play cards, or hang out with "his family." Chris said it was just how his family was. He said if I just accepted that, his family would eventually warm up to me. They never really did though.

Q: How did you feel around his family?

A: Actually, I never really felt comfortable around Chris's family—especially around Chris's brother Willie. Willie drank too much and made me feel uncomfortable around him. One time, at a family picnic, both Willie and Chris had been drinking. They'd gone off together for a while, leaving me to help Chris's mom and cousins to clean up. When Chris and Willie returned, I smelled the faint odor of marijuana on them both. No one else seemed to notice. No one said a word. On the way home, when I asked Chris about it, he became angry with me. He left the house and did not come home for three days. When Chris returned, we never spoke about it again. In order to maintain peace in our home I accepted that I would never question Chris's behaviors around his family again, so long as Chris continued to treat me with respect.

Q: Did there come a time when Chris' work situation changed? Tell us about that.
A: About two years after we married, Chris's shifts became erratic at work. He was working long hours, two shifts a day. Although I missed spending time with him, he said the money was too good to pass up. He said it would help us save money and buy a large home.
Q: How did all these extra hours affect your family life?
A: The hours began to take their toll on Chris, I guess on me, too. He became resentful, and angry, he told me he had changed his mind about having children. He said he didn't want to feel "tied down"—I was devastated. Although we had been using protection and had agreed to wait until I was tenured to start a family, we had always planned to have children. Around this time I accidentally got pregnant. Chris became distant and angry at first, but one day, just seemed to "snap out of it."
Q: What happened next?
A: We bought a spacious three-bedroom home in an upper-class neighborhood in Pelican Bay, West Calusa Hills on Lullaby Lane, just before our first daughter, Ariel, was born. About two years later, I gave birth to our second daughter, Jasmine. Chris adored them. Even though Chris still worked long hours and came home late at night at least three or four

times a week, he seemed a changed man. Chris was a devoted husband and father.
Q: Why did you have an alarm system at your house?
A: Shortly after we moved into our new home, we contracted with PDQ to install a monitored alarm system. Having the system made me feel much more secure, given that Chris's work hours sometimes involved his coming home late.
Q: Were there any weapons in the home?
A: Chris had a gun. Because Chris won't buy a gun safe, I make him keep it in the laundry room—on a high shelf out of the girl's sight and reach. It's the only way I can forget it's there and not worry about it being in the home.
Q: Why did you get life insurance on your husband recently?
A: One of Chris' friends put us in contact with Sharon Barry, a Friends Helping Friends (FHF) Insurance agent. Sharon set up a meeting with us, and agreed to come to our home to accommodate Chris's schedule. Sharon recommended we purchase a $250,000 policy, based on what we could afford at the time. A part of the insurance policy was assigned to pay funeral costs in the event of one of our deaths. We felt that this policy, plus the group policy Chris had through IMF would be more than ample to cover our family's needs.
Q: I would like to draw your attention now the night your husband was murdered. Do you remember that night?

A: I remember the night Chris was killed. I remember pieces—some of it is vivid and clear in my mind. Other parts of it are fragmented.
Q: Please explain.
A: June 3, 200x-2 was a Thursday evening. School had let out for the summer a few weeks earlier. Around 10:00 PM, I received a call from my niece, Lilli Duke. We discussed our plans to meet for lunch the next day and only talked about one minute. After hanging up the phone, I went to check on the girls. They were sound asleep. The girls are like their father—they can sleep through a live marching band playing in their bedroom. Although I don't specifically remember checking the alarm before going to bed, it was usually my habit to do so. I hate being alone in the house with the girls when Chris isn't home.
Q: What did you do next?
A: I took a bath and got ready for bed. I think I was asleep by 10:30—bathing relaxes me. I have always been an early bird, but something of a light sleeper. Chris usually slept in the den when he got home late so he wouldn't wake me. Chris wasn't home by the time I fell asleep.
Q: Did you stay asleep?
A: No, something startled me awake. I am still not certain if I know exactly what it was. At first, I thought the noise might be the air conditioner outside our bedroom window. The

fan and motor always makes noise when it kicks on, sort of like a clack, loud hum, and then a pop, pop, pop. It drives Chris crazy. I've learned to sleep through it or ignore it.
Q: What was the noise?
A: I don't know, but I don't think it was the air conditioner. At least I don't think so. Before I realized what was happening, I was in the living room. I saw Chris's body on the floor. The alarm was sounding. The front door was open. Chris was half dressed. He was not moving. I think I screamed. I remember yelling at him—pounding on him to wake up. I did not move from Chris's side. I think I was there when the police arrived. It felt like an eternity. Later, I learned it only took them a few minutes to arrive.
Q: What happened after the police arrived?
A: I don't really remember, I just remember questions being asked of me. After I knew the girls were safe, I just zoned out. There were police and technicians all over our home. It was noisy. I don't even know what I was thinking, other than I wanted to go somewhere safe with my girls. I remember vaguely that the police asked me about guns in the house. I think I told them there were no guns because I had forgotten about the one in the laundry room. When the police showed me a holster they found under the bed, I remembered the gun in the laundry room and took them to it.
Q: How long did this questioning by the police last?

A: I'm not real sure, but after several hours, the police allowed me, Ariel, and Jasmine to leave the house with my brother. The police didn't search me before leaving, but, later, they called me back to the house and tested my hands and arms for gunpowder. The test turned out a single speck of gunpowder on the back of my left hand. Even though I told the police I did not kill my husband and that I was right-handed, they did not seem to believe me. I was arrested for the murder of my husband, Chris Alexander. My life, as I had once known it to be, ended forever.
Q: Ms. Alexander did you kill you husband?
A: No.
Q: Well if you didn't whom do you suspect?
A: I think it might have been that "lady" Nikki Long, she was mad because Chris had broken things off with her and come back home to me and the girls. He always came back to us. She had been talking crap around town about how she was going to take my man and I know that sort of stuff embarrasses his family - you just don't want to make them mad.
Q: Nothing further, Your Honor.

-Notes-

Name Chris Alexander	**Sex** M	**Hour of Death** 2300 hours	**Date of Death** **6/6/20XX-2**
Race Other	**Age** 36	**DOB** 10/22/20XX-36	**County of Death** Calusa
SSN 555-45-3244	**Marital Status** Married	**Surviving Spouse** Brandi Alexander	**State of Death** XX

Residence-State XXXXXXX	**Residence-County** Calusa	**Residence-City** Pelican Bay	**Street Address** 6731 Lullaby Lane

Father Willie Alexander	**Mother** Frances Alexander	**Address(es):** 9123 South St., Pelican Bay, XX 33465

Informant's Name Brandi Alexander	**Mailing Address:** 6731 Lullaby Lane, Pelican Bay, XX 33707

Disposition: Buried	**Cemetery/Crematorium** Happy Acres	**Location:** Pelican Bay	**Medical Examiner:** Dr. Jeremiah Jones, M.E

Funeral Home: Happy Acres	**Mailing Address:** P.O. Box 345, Pelican Bay, XX 33902

Person who pronounced death: Dr. Jeremiah Jones County Coroner/Medical Examiner	**Pronounced Dead on:** 6/6/20XX-2	**Location:** Calusa County Hospital 1921 Sherman Way Pelican Bay, XX 33450

Coroner: Dr. Jeremiah Jones	**Mailing Address:** Calusa County Hospital 1921 Sherman Way, Pelican Bay, XX 33450

Cause of Death: Internal injuries from gunshot wounds to the chest and groin. Victim bled to death	**Signature of Coroner:** Dr. Jeremiah Jones, M.E.

Other Significant Conditions: 4 non-lethal gunshot wounds	**Autopsy:** Yes	**Was Case Referred to Medical Examiner:** Yes

Accident/Suicide/Homicide/Other: Homicide	**Means of Death:** Gunshot wounds, Loss of Blood

Place of Death: Home	**Address:** 6731 Lullaby Lane Pelican Bay, XX 33707

OFFICE OF THE MEDICAL EXAMINER
CALUSA COUNTY

Jeremiah Jones, M.D.
Eric Kilhim, M.D.
Carol Morbid, M.D.
505 South Morte Circle
Pelican Bay, XX 33333
(505) 555-0001

NAME:	Chris Alexander	**AUTOPSY NO:**	00XX-2-767
SEX:	Male	**DATE OF AUTOPSY:**	Jun 8, 00XX-2
RACE:	White	**TIME OF AUTOPSY:**	10:15 a.m.
AGE:	36	**PATHOLOGIST:**	Jeremiah Jones, M.D.
DOB:	10/22/1771		Chief Medical Examiner

FINAL PATHOLOGICAL DIAGNOSES:

I. MASSIVE HEMORHAGING FROM SEVERED RIGHT FEMORAL ARTERY

II. MASSIVE HEMORRHAGE FROM SEVERED LEFT FEMORAL ARTERY

III. HEMORRHAGE IN RIGHT ANTERIOR GROIN AREA

IV. HEMORHAGE IN LEFT ANTERIOR GROIN AREA

V. HEMORRHAGE IN LEFT CENTRAL CHEST AREA

CAUSE OF DEATH: MULTIPLE GUNSHOT WOUNDS TO THE GROIN AREA

MANNER OF DEATH: HOMICIDE

Dr. Jeremiah Jones, M.D.
Jeremiah Jones, M.D.
Chief Medical Examiner

CLOTHING:

The body has a pair of boxer underwear on, soaked with blood in the groin area. No other clothing items. No jewelry.

EXTERNAL EXAMINATION:

The body is that of a well-developed, well-nourished white male appearing the offered age of 38 years old. The body measures 74 feet and weighs 195 pounds.

The unembalmed body is well preserved and cool to touch due to refrigeration. Rigor mortis is developing in the major muscle groups. Liver mortis is fixed and purple posteriorly except over pressure points. During initial examination, there was no rigor and lividity was at a minimum and unfixed.

There are six gun shot wounds. All six wounds enter the body in the anterior and exit the body in the posterior. Two wounds are in the right chest area and four in the groin area. The wounds are described in detail below.

The scalp hair is black and measures up to 4 inches in length in the fontal area and up to 3 inches in the back and on top of the head. The irises are black and the pupils are dilated with redness. The teeth are natural and in good condition. The fenula are intact. The oral mucosa and tongue are free of injuries. The external ears have no injuries.

The neck is symmetrical and shows no masses or injuries. The trachea is in the midline. The shoulders are symmetrical and are free of scars.

The flat abdomen has no injuries. The back is symmetrical. The buttocks are unremarkable.

The fingernails are short and clean.

OTHER IDENTIFYING FEATURES:

There is one scar and one tattoo on the body.

SCAR:
There is ¼ inch scar on the top right arm anterior of the elbow.

TATTOOS:
There is one tattoo of the word "Frosty" on the right arm posterior of the shoulder. There is another tattoo of a marijuana leaf on the left arm posterior of the shoulder.

INTERNAL EXAMINATION:

The body was opened with the usual Y incision. The left chest and groin areas displayed significant trauma from gun shots. Otherwise, unremarkable.

BODY CAVITIES:

The muscles of the right chest were normal and the muscles of the left chest were torn and traumatized form the gun shots. The lungs were atelectatic when the pleural cavities were opened. The ribs, sternum and spine exhibit no fractures. The right pleural cavity was free of fluid. The left pleural cavity contained a moderate amount of blood. The pericardial sac has a normal amount of clear yellow fluid. The diaphragm has no abnormality. The subcutaneous abdominal fat measures 5 centimeters in thickness at the umbilicus. The abdominal cavity is lined with glistening serosa and has no collections of free fluid. The organs are normally situated. The mesentery and omentum are unremarkable.

NECK:

The soft tissues and the strap muscles of the neck exhibit no abnormalities. The hyoid bone and the cartilages and the larynx and thyroid are intact and show no evidence of injury. The larynx and trachea are lined by smooth pink-tan mucosa, are patent and contain no foreign matter. The epiglottis and vocal cords are unremarkable. The cervical verbal column is intact. The carotid arteries and jugular veins are unremarkable.

CARDIOVASCULAR SYSTEM:

The heart and great vessels contain dark red liquid blood and little postmortem clots. The heart weighs 308 grams. The epicedial surface has normal amount of glistening, yellow adipose tissue. The coronary arteries are free of atherosclerosis.

The pulmonary trunk and arteries are opened in situ and there is no evidence of thromboemboli. The intimal surface of the aorta is smooth with a few scattered yellow atheromata. The ostia of the major branches are normal distribution and dimension. The inferior vena cava and tributaries have no antemortem clots.

RESIRATORY SYSTEM:

The lungs weigh 555 grams and 552 grams, right and left respectively. There is a small amount of subpleural anthracotic pigment within the lobes. The pleural surfaces are free of exudates: right-sided pleural adhesions have been described above. The trachea and bonchi have smooth tan epithelium. The cut surfaces of the lungs are red-pin and have mild edema. The lung parenchyma is of the usual consistency and shows no evidence of neoplasm, consolidation, thromboemboli, fibrosis o calcification.

HEPATOBILIAY SYSTEM:

The liver weighs 2545 grams. The liver edge is somewhat blunted. The capsule is intact. The cut surfaces are red-brown and normal consistency. There are no focal lesions. The gallbladder contains 15 milliliters of dark green bile. There are no stones. The mucosa is unremarkable. The large bile ducts are patent and non-dilated.

HEMOLYMPHATIC SYSTEM:

The thymus is not identified. The spleen weighs 305 grams. The capsule is shiny, smooth and intact. The cut surfaces are firm and moderately congested. The lymphoid tissue in the spleen is within a normal range. The lymph nodes throughout the body are no enlarged.

GASTROINTESTINAL SYSTEM:

The tongue shows a small focus of sub mucosal hemorrhage near the tip. The esophagus is empty and the mucosa is unremarkable. The stomach contains an estimated 29 milliliters of thick sanguinous fluid. The gastric mucosa shows no evidence of ulceration. There is a mild flattening of the rugal pattern within the antrum with intense hyperemia. The duodenum contains bile-stained hick tan fluid. The jejunum, ileum, and the colon contain yellowish fluid with a thick, cloudy, particulate matter. There is no major alteration to internal and external inspection and palpitation except for a yellowish/white shiny discoloration of the mucosa. The vermiform appendix is identified. The pancreas is tan, lobulated and shows no neoplasia calcification or hemorrhage.

There are no intraluminal masses or pseudomenbrane.

UROGENITAL SYSTEM:

The kindeys are similar size and shape and weigh 159 grams and 176 grams, right and left, respectively. The capsules are intact and strip with ease. The cortical surfaces are purplish, congested and mildly granular. The cut surfaces reveal a well-defined corticomedullary unction. There are no structural abnormalities of the medullae, calyces or pelvis. The ureters are slender and patent. The urinary bladder has approximately 0.5 milliliters of cloudy yellow urine. The mucosa is unremarkable.

The penis and testes appear normal.

ENDOKRINE SYSTEM:

The adrenal glands have a normal configuration with the golden yellow cotices well demarcated from the underlying medullae and there is no evidence of hemorrhage. The thyroid gland is mildly fibrotic and has vocally pale gray parenchyma on sectioning. The pituitary gland is within normal limits.

MUSCULOSKELETAL SYTEM:

Postmortem radiographs of the body show no acute, healed or healing fractures of the head, neck appendicular skeleton or the axial skeleton. The muscles are normally formed.

CENTRAL NERVOUS SYSTEM:

The scalp has no hemorrhage or contusions. The calvarium is intact. There is no epidural, subdural or subarachnoid hemorrhage. The brain has a normal convolutional pattern and weighs 1270 grams. The meninges are clear. The cortical surfaces of the brain have mild to moderate flattening of the gyri with narrowing of the sulci.

EVIDENCE OF INJURIES:

There are six gunshot wounds. These are given Roman Numeral designations; however these designations are random and do not correspond to the degree of severity of injuries, nor to the sequence in which they have been inflicted.

I. Perforating gunshot wound of right upper chest:

An entrance gunshot wound is located on the decedent's right upper chest, 2 inches to the right of the right nipple. It is a 1/4 inch circular perforation with a symmetrical 1/8 inch dark margin of abrasion. No soot or stippling is seen in association with this wound.

After perforating the skin and soft tissues of the right chest, the bullet enters the right chest wall at the 5th intercostals space and subsequently fractures ribs #6-9, posterior-laterally and exits behind the right posterior chest wall through the 8th intercostal space. Powder residue is not visible in the wound track. There is moderate tissue disruption along the bullet track. There is no major or minor injury to any organ from this wound. No bullet is recovered.

This was an indeterminate/distant range perforating gunshot wound of the right chest which passes front to back, slightly left, and slightly downward.

II. Perforating gunshot wound of right lower chest:

An entrance gunshot wound is located in the decedent's right lower chest, 2 inches below and 1 inch to the right of the right nipple. It is a 1/4 inch round perforation with an asymmetric margin of abrasion which measures 1/4 inch at the superior aspect of the wound and 1/8 inch at the inferior aspect of the wound. No soot or stippling is seen in association with this wound.

After perforating the skin and soft tissues of the left lateral chest, the bullet enters the abdominal cavity via the 8th intercostals space, injures multiple loops of small bowel and penetrates the retroperitoneal soft tissues of the upper left pelvis. The bullet exits the left lower back. Powder residue is not visible in the wound track. There is slight tissue disruption along the bullet track. No bullet is recovered.

This was an indeterminate/distant range gunshot wound of the right chest which passes front to back and downward.

III. Perforating gunshot wounds of left groin:

There are two entrance gunshot wounds in the decedent's left pelvis area.

a. The first wound in the left groin area is located 1 inch to the left of the pubis. It is a 1/4 inch circular perforation with a symmetrical 1/8 inch dark margin of abrasion. No soot or stippling is seen in association with this wound. After perforating the skin, the wound extends through the muscles and soft tissues of the abdomen and punctures the prostate gland. The bullet perforates the psoas muscle and exits the body to the left of the sacrum.

b. The second wound in the left groin area is located 2 inches to the left of the pubis. It is a 1/4 inch circular perforation with a symmetrical 1/8 inch dark margin of abrasion. No soot or stippling is seen in association with this wound. After perforating the skin, the wound extends through the muscles and soft tissue of the abdomen and perforates the femoral artery. The bullet exits the body through the gluteus maximus to the left of the sacrum.

These are indeterminate/distant range gunshot wounds of the left groin which pass from front to back.

IV. Perforating gunshot wounds of right groin:

There are two gunshot wounds in the decedent's right pelvis area.

a. The first wound is in the right groin area located 1 and ¼ inches to the right of the pubis. It is a 1/4 inch circular perforation with a symmetrical 1/8 inch dark margin of abrasion. No soot or stippling is seen in association with this wound. After perforating the skin, the wound extends through the muscles and soft tissues of the abdomen and punctures the bladder. The bullet exits the body through the gluteus maximus to the right of the sacrum.

b. The second wound is in the right groin area located 3 inches to the right of the pubis. It is a 1/4 inch circular perforation with a symmetrical 1/8 inch dark margin of abrasion. No soot or stippling is seen in association with this wound. After perforating the skin, the wound extends through the muscles and soft tissues of the abdomen and punctures the right femoral artery. The bullet exits through the gluteus maximus to the left of the sacrum.

These are indeterminate/distant range gunshot wounds of the left groin which pass from front to back.

Enclosure 1 – Autopsy Diagram
Enclosure 2 – Blank Body Diagram

ST/GPS/lsr

Dictated: 06/08/00XX-2
Transcribed: 06/09/00XX-2
Finalized: 06/15/00XX-2

Enclosure 1

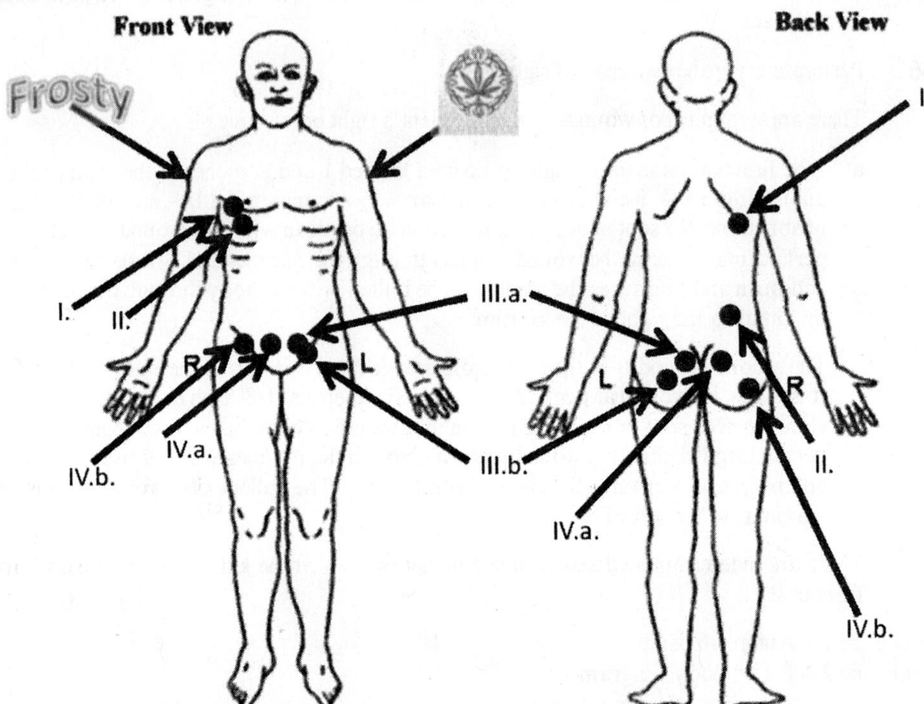
Front View
Back View
Frosty
I.
II.
III.a.
III.b.
IV.a.
IV.b.
R
L
I.
III.a.
L
R
II.
III.b.
IV.a.
IV.b.
Autopsy Notes: Chris Alexander, conducted 06/09/20XX-2 J.J. ME

Enclosure 2

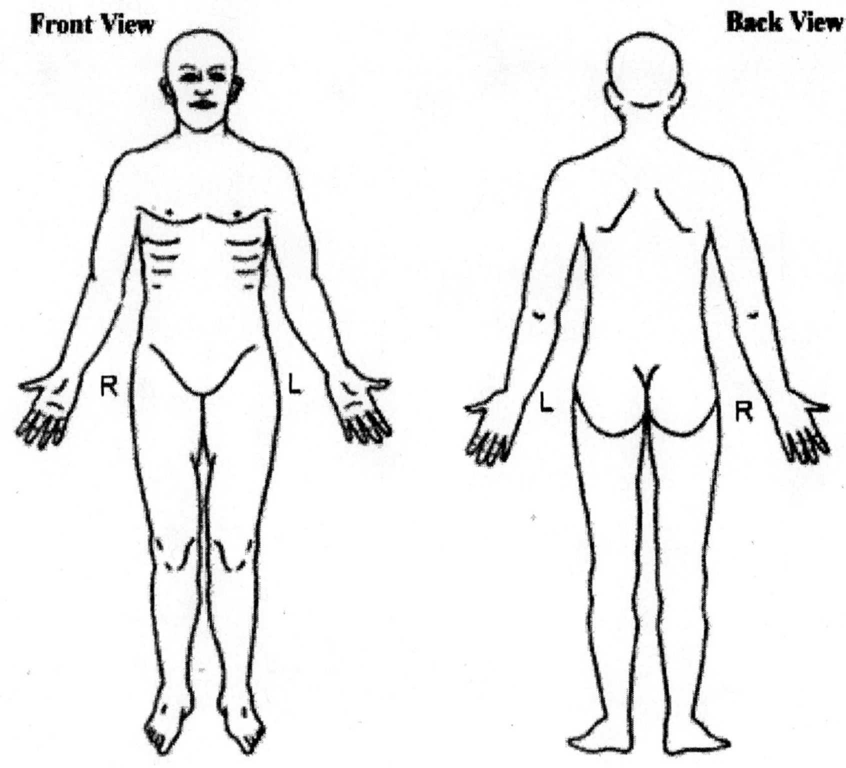

EVIDENCE

Agency:	Pelican Bay Police Department		Calusa County
Collected By:	Officer Anece Baxter-White		
Item Number:		Case Number:	20XX(-2)1959
Date:	6-6-20XX-2	Time:	2345 hours

Description: Small Bag of white powder, field test positive for presence of cocaine, identified as exhibit 9 in the case file.

Remarks: Secured properly, carried to station and turned over to the evidence custodian.

CHAIN OF CUSTODY

Received From: Officer Anece Baxter-White *Anece Baxter-White*
Received By: Detective William Murphy *Bill Murphy*
Date: 6-7-20XX(-2) Time: 0239 HOURS

Received From: Detective William Murphy – by Certified Mail
Received By: Doctor Steven Schwarz, Calusa County Forensic Laboratory *Felix Schwarz*
Date: 7-23-20XX(-2) Time: 0932 Hours

Received From: Calusa County, Forensic Laboratory –by Certified Mail
Received By: Detective William Murphy *Bill Murphy*
Date: 10-10-20XX(-2) Time: 1232 Hours

EVIDENCE

Agency: Pelican Bay Police Department — Calusa County
Collected By: Officer Scott Frost
Item Number: — Case Number: 20XX(-2)1959
Date: 6-6-20XX-2 — Time: 0232 hours

Description: Small Bag of green leafy substance, field test positive for presence of marijuana, identified as exhibit 10 in the case file.

Remarks: Secured properly, carried to station and turned over to the evidence custodian.

CHAIN OF CUSTODY

Received From: Officer Scott Frost *Scott Frost*
Received By: Detective William Murphy *Bill Murphy*
Date: 6-7-20XX(-2) Time: 0339 HOURS

Received From: Detective William Murphy – by Certified Mail
Received By: Doctor Steven Schwarz, Calusa County Forensic Laboratory *Felix Schwarz*
Date: 7-23-20XX(-2) Time: 0932 Hours

Received From: Calusa County, Forensic Laboratory –by Certified Mail
Received By: Detective William Murphy *Bill Murphy*
Date: 10-10-20XX(-2) Time: 1232 Hours

CALUSA COUNTY FORENSIC LABORATORY
415 COUNTY ROAD 369
CALUSA COUNTY, FLORIDA 33459

August 4, 20XX-2

Page 1 of 1

DRUG CHEMISTRY DIVISION REPORT

SUBJECT: **Submitter Case Number: 20XX(-2)-9x-PBPD454**
Laboratory Referral Number: 20XX(-2)-948
Subject: Chris Alexander

Exhibits:

1 1 plastic bag containing white powder (Item 1)
2 1 plastic bag containing green leafy substance (Item 2)

Findings:
Examination of white powder material in Exhibit 1 revealed the presence of cocaine. Amounts (grams):

Exhibit	Received	Used	Returned
1	45.0	0.5	44.5

Examination of green leafy substance material in Exhibit 2 revealed the presence of marijuana. Amounts (grams):

Exhibit	Received	Used	Returned
2	154.0	1.0	153.0

Stephen F. Schwarz, M.D.
Stephen F. Schwarz, Ph.D.
Forensic Chemist

CERTIFICATE

I certify that I am the custodian of records of the Calusa County Forensic Laboratory, and that the foregoing is a true copy of the record of this Laboratory.

James Holder, M.D.
JAMES HOLDER, M.D.
Director, Calusa County Forensic Laboratory

-Notes-

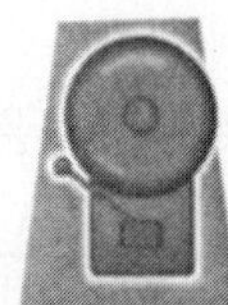

PDQ Alarm Systems, Inc.,
2914 49th Avenue South
Pelican Bay, XX 33606
727-555-9012

Mr. Christopher Alexander
6731 Lullaby Lane
Pelican Bay, XX 33707

Dear Sir/Ma'am:

In accordance with your *PDQ* Alarm system plan we are writing to inform you of the reported activity for your system during the time period May 15, 20XX-2 through June 15, 20XX-2. A review of the computer logs maintained on our system provides the following information:

Date:	Incident:	Action Taken:
20XX-2.05.16.2139	Alarm tripped – garage door	Called home IAW plan requirements. Homeowner Alexander answered phone call and indicated he had just come in through the garage and forgot to reset the system.
20XX-2.05.23.1649	Alarm tripped – front door	Called home IAW plan requirements. Homeowner's wife said children went out the door before the system was disarmed. Explained the fact that there is no lag time between opening of door and tripping of alarm.
20XX-2.06.06.2253	Alarm tripped – front door	Called home IAW plan requirements. Wife on the phone saying someone shot husband, send help. Very upset, almost incomprehensible. Called Police through 911 system and reported incident.

As always we appreciate your business and look forward to providing for all of your security related needs in the future.

Sincerely,

Russell Martin

Russell Martin
CEO, PDQ Alarm Systems

Individual Charges

www.sprintpcs.com

Customer	Account Number	Invoice Period	Page
Chris Alexander	0166000555-3	May 31 – Jun 30	5 of 16

Individual Charges for Chris Alexander (continued)
727-555-2260
cafrostie@sprintpcs.com

Voice Call Detail

Date	Time	Phone Number	Call Destination	Rate/ Type	Minutes Used	Airtime Charges	LD/Additional Charges	Total Charges
5.31	1739	555-3624	Pelican Bay		7	included	0.00	0.00
5.31	1943	555-3461	Incoming		2	included	0.00	0.00
6.1	1345	555-3327	Pelican Bay		12	included	0.00	0.00
6.1	1603	555-3463	Jacksonville		3	included	0.00	0.00
6.1	1954	555-3461	Incoming		2	included	0.00	0.00
6.2	1433	555-6633	Pelican Bay		15	included	0.00	0.00
6.2	1729	555-3624	Pelican Bay		29	included	0.00	0.00
6.3	2012	555-3327	Pelican Bay		5	included	0.00	0.00
6.3	2213	555-1623	Incoming		2	included	0.00	0.00
6.5	2312	555-3463	Jacksonville		4	included	0.00	0.00
6.6	1501	01934-679	Juarez, Mx		2	included	0.00	0.00
6.6	1515	555-1623	Incoming		2	included	0.00	0.00
6.6	1621	555-3461	Incoming		2	included	0.00	0.00
6.6	1752	01934-679	Mexico City, Mx		2	included	0.00	0.00
6.6	2201	555-5172	Pelican Bay		4	included	0.00	0.00
6.6	2210	555-3624	Pelican Bay		23	included	0.00	0.00

- PCS Calling

EM Notes:
555-5172 – Alexander Home Number
555-3327 – Brandi Alexander Cell Phone
555-3624 – Nikki Long Cell Phone
555-6633 – Nikki's Hair Salon

Doctor Horrible

The Pelican Bay Star

November 3, 20XX-2
By Phillip Payne, State Court Correspondent

In January, the State Supreme Court took an unusual step. In the murder trial of 14-year-old Danny Wayne Morris, the court tossed out the testimony of the medical examiner who had conducted the autopsy of the body.

Why you may ask? The medical examiner in the case, Dr. Jeremiah Jones, had testified under oath that he could tell from the bullet wounds in the body that Morris and his brother simultaneously held the gun to fire the fatal shot. Unfortunately it is impossible to make such a determination from examining bullet wounds, a point the Supreme Court explained at length in their opinion.

Former Pelican Bay Police Chief B.J. Mills has been trying for years to draw attention to Dr. Jones. "There's no question in my mind that there are innocent people doing time due to the testimony of Dr. Jones," he says. "I reckon some may even be on death row."

Over the twenty years that Dr. Jones has been a medical examiner state Supreme Court justices, police officers, defense lawyers, crime lab experts and other state medical examiners have made public their concerns with his practice at one time or another.

Although Dr. Jones refused to speak talk with the paper, he did make the following observation on the witness stand during the Morris trial. He claimed under oath to perform anywhere from 1,500 to 1,800 autopsies a year. The National Association of Medical Examiners (NAME) says a medical examiner should perform no more than 250 autopsies per year. After 325, the organization refuses to certify an examiner's practice.

"That number cannot be done," says Antonio DeMarossa, author of The Complete Guide to Forensic Pathology, widely considered the guiding textbook. "After 250 autopsies, you start making small mistakes. At 300, you're going to get mental and physical strains on your body. Over 350, and you're talking about major fatigue and major mistakes."

For much of his career Dr. Jones, 71, has conducted autopsies as well as held two research and hospital positions and testified in court two to four times per week. After reviewing one Jones autopsy in a 2003 homicide case, Dr. James McDonald, who sits on NAME's ethics committee, sent a strongly-worded letter to the defendant's attorney describing Dr. Jones's conclusions as "near-total speculation," the quality of his report "pathetic." As a result of Dr. McDonald's letter, the prosecutor dropped the murder charge and the defendant pleaded guilty to the lesser charge of manslaughter.

Another medical examiner reviewed Dr. Jones's autopsy in a 1998 homicide and characterized his work as "near complete malpractice." In that case, Dr. Jones had determined that a woman had died of "natural causes." The diagnosis was later changed to homicide by blunt force to the head. According to the medical examiner that performed the second autopsy, Dr. Jones hadn't even emptied the woman's pockets, a standard autopsy procedure. No one has been prosecuted in the case. Dr. Jones declined repeated requests from me to comment.

Dr. Jones isn't a board-certified forensic pathologist, at least as the term is understood by his peers. The American Board of Pathology is considered the only reputable certifying organization for forensic pathology. Dr. Jones failed the board's exam in the 1980s. He still testifies in court that he's "board certified." But that's a reference to his membership in the American Academy of Forensic Examiners, which he has said publicly certified him without requiring him to take an exam.

Part of the problem is a lack of oversight. Elected county coroners and district attorneys shop out autopsies to private-practice medical examiners. The county pays doctors $550 for each autopsy, plus extra for other tests and services. Dr. Jones has dominated these referrals for years, a strong indication that coroners and district attorneys are happy with his work. And the state Supreme Court, although it tossed out his testimony in the Morris case, didn't stop him from testifying in other cases. Most experts agree that a medical examiner should be independent and find facts irrespective of their value to the prosecution.

Consider William Schifflett, convicted and sentenced to death in 2002 for the murder of his girlfriend's infant daughter. The indigent Schifflett asked the trial court for money to hire his own expert to review Dr. Jones's findings -- a crucial part of the state's case. He was denied. Schifflett's attorneys were able to get a former state medical examiner from a neighboring state to review Dr. Jones's autopsy for his appeal. Though the second autopsy raised real doubts about Schifflett's guilt, the state Supreme Court declined to even consider it, ruling that it was new evidence, and should have been introduced at trial.

That's not an uncommon ruling from an appellate court, but it illustrates just how important it is that state expert witnesses be reputable, credible, and accountable before ever stepping onto the witness stand.

Our state leaders should put an immediate end to Dr. Jones's autopsy operation. The state also needs to revisit every criminal case in which Dr. Jones has testified. Finally, we need to implement significant reforms as to how autopsies are conducted – we could start by requiring all contracted medical examiners to at least meet the profession's minimum standards. Until then, a cloud of suspicion hangs over every murder conviction that comes out of the state's courts.

DA Argues Infidelity, Money Motivated Killing

The Pelican Bay Star

December 7, 20XX-1

By Phillip Payne, State Court Correspondent

Pelican Bay -- Prosecutors are honing in on infidelity and money as reasons a former teacher might have killed her husband in 20XX-2.

Chris Alexander was shot six times in his living room, and his wife, Brandi, told police she believed he was killed after answering the front door.

Police recovered several .45 caliber shell casings in the foyer, outside the front door and in the flowerbed. But the only blood found in the house was under Chris Alexander in the living room.

Brandi Alexander also had traces of gunshot residue on her left hand. The defense plans to argue that it came from touching her husband's body.

The prosecution claims Brandi Alexander was angry about her husband's affair with another woman who spoke with him just minutes before he was killed.

That woman, Nikki Long, took the stand Wednesday afternoon and said she was on the phone with Chris Alexander for 30 minutes just moments before he was shot. Long said he had to hang up because his wife came in the room.

The district attorney told the jury that Brandi Alexander killed her husband for a $250,000 life insurance policy and because she found out he had at least two mistresses.

The former Public School teacher was arrested and charged in the slaying a week later.

Detective: Suspect Lied Night of Husband's Death

The Pelican Bay Star

December 9, 20XX-1
By Phillip Payne, State Court Correspondent

Pelican Bay -- Testimony in the second day of a former teacher's murder trial revealed that she lied to police on the night of her husband's slaying.

Officer Anece Baxter White told jurors Thursday that Brandi Alexander lied to her about a gun being in the couple's house. Only after she told her an empty gun holster was found under her bed did the Public School teacher say there was a .9-millimeter in the garage, Baxter White testified.

A friend of the victim, Chris Alexander, said in court that Alexander had owned a .45-caliber gun that is still missing -- the same type of gun used to kill Alexander.

An investigator testified he found no signs of forced entry or blood anywhere in the house except around the body of Chris Alexander. A neighbor who lives across the street also told the jury he heard gunshots the night of the killing, looked out and saw no one leave the Alexander house.

An aunt of Chris Alexander that went to the house the night of the crime testified that Brandi Alexander had gone into a bathroom to wash up. She later tested positive for gunshot residue on the back of her left hand.

Brandi Alexander was arrested and charged in the slaying a week after her husband's death.

Teacher's Attorney Blasts Investigation: Defense Claims Detective Left Details Out Of Report

The Pelican Bay Star

December 13, 20XX-2
By Phillip Payne, State Court Correspondent

Pelican Bay -- The defense for a former Public Schools teacher blasted police during her murder trial Monday, saying detectives did a sloppy and incomplete investigation.

Lead Detective Ed Morris spent most of the day on the stand telling jurors what Brandi Alexander told him about the night of her husband's death and defending his own report.

Defense attorney Ross Eastman ripped into Morris, claiming he'd left out details in his initial report that he included in his testimony -- facts such as inaccurate dates and who was at the crime scene the night of the slaying.

Morris told jurors he interviewed Brandi Alexander six days after the killing and that she had several inconsistencies in her story, mainly about the couple's security system. Alexander first said she heard the alarm go off while she was sleeping, then heard popping noises, Morris testified. But he said Alexander changed the story moments later, saying the popping sounds came first.

Brandi Alexander claims she found her husband shot on the living room floor and that someone else did it. She tested positive for gunshot residue, and there were no signs of forced entry or blood anywhere in the house except around the body.

Teacher's Murder Trial Resumes

The Pelican Bay Star

January 2, 20XX-1
By Phillip Payne, State Court Correspondent

Pelican Bay -- Testimony is expected to continue Thursday morning in the trial of a Public School teacher accused of killing her husband. Opening statements began Wednesday in the case.

The defense claims someone else shot Brandi Alexander' husband Chris as he answered their front door in June 20XX-2.

But the prosecution claims she killed her husband to collect a $250,000 life insurance policy. Prosecutors said Brandi Alexander was angry about her husband's affairs with two other women.

In court on Wednesday, one of those women claimed she spoke with Chris Alexander just minutes before he was killed.

Police recovered several .45 caliber shell casings in the house.

Brandi Alexander also had traces of gunshot residue on her left hand. The defense said that was because she touched her husband's body.

Juror Dismissed In Ex-Teacher's Murder Trial

The Pelican Bay Star

January 4, 20XX-1
By Phillip Payne, State Court Correspondent

Pelican Bay -- A juror was dismissed Friday in the murder trial of a former Public Schools teacher.

Brandi Alexander is accused of killing her husband, Chris Alexander, at their home.

Juror No. 5 was dismissed because she had been taking medication and was seen closing her eyes and not focusing on testimony Thursday.

The jury now has eight white members and four black members -- three of them women. Judge Jerry Parker noted a defense objection and moved forward.

Much of Friday's testimony focused on shell casings and bullet fragments in the house. Alexander was shot six times and died in his living room. Although the shell casings were found outside the front door, most of the bullet fragments were around and underneath the body.

The prosecution contended Brandi Alexander stood over her husband's body and shot him, sending bullets into the concrete underneath the living room carpet -- something a gun expert from the state crime lab said is possible.

Brandi Alexander claimed someone at their front door shot her husband while she was in the bedroom. She tested positive for traces of gunshot residue on the back of her left hand, investigators said.

The trial has ended for the weekend. Alexander could be sentenced to life in prison if she's found guilty.

Teacher Guilty!

The Pelican Bay Star

January 9, 20XX-1
By Phillip Payne, State Court Correspondent

It took a Calusa County Jury only two hours to reach a guilty verdict in Brandi Alexander's Alexander' murder trial.

"We the jury, find the defendant guilty as charged," read the court foreman.

Brandi Alexander showed no emotion Tuesday after she was found guilty of the 200XX-2 killing of her husband, Chris Alexander.

Chris Alexander' father said the verdict does little to numb his pain.

"I'm pleased with what the verdict was. I'm not happy, but pleased, because God confirmed what he showed me two and a half years ago," Chris Alexander Sr. said.

Chris Alexander was shot six times in the living room of the north Jackson home he shared with his wife in June 20XX-2. The gun has never been found.

During the trial, prosecutors alleged that Brandi Alexander killed her husband because he had two mistresses and also to cash in on a $250,000 life insurance policy.

Prosecutors also claimed gunshot residue found on her hand proved she fired the shots.

Defense attorneys called only one witness. The defense contended that Brandi Alexander was asleep in her bedroom when her husband was fatally shot and that she discovered his body after hearing popping noises.

"There's no direct evidence. There's not one piece of direct evidence you can seize or put your hands on and say 'I'm convinced beyond a reasonable doubt.' They build inference onto inference, and the law doesn't allow that," defense attorney Ross Eastman said.

After the verdict was read, Brandi Alexander' family members cried in the courtroom and did not want to speak as they left the courthouse.

Her attorneys said they will request a new trial.

Since the murder, Chris Alexander' family has continued a limited relationship with Brandi because of the couple's children.

Chris Alexander' father said he still questions why his son was murdered.

"When someone tells you point blank, 'I didn't have anything to do with your son's death,' and come to find out that person lied to you, that hurts. It really hurts." Mr. Alexander said.

Judge Jerry Parker sentenced Brandi Alexander to life in prison shortly after she was found guilty.

Retrial Set For Teacher Charged With Murder

The Pelican Bay Star

By Phillip Payne, State Court Correspondent

Pelican Bay -- A former public school teacher accused of killing her husband will be retried this week.

Brandi Alexander' retrial originally was scheduled for May, but attorneys for both sides said scheduling conflicts forced them to set a November date.

During her first trial, prosecutors claimed she killed Chris Alexander to cash in on a life insurance policy and because he had two mistresses.

Alexander was convicted in January and sentenced to life in prison, but that verdict was thrown out after Judge Jerry Parker ruled that prosecutors sought to keep blacks off the jury.

She was released on $150,000 bond.

The retrial starts Tuesday.

-Notes-

State of XXXXX
UNIFORM COMMITMENT TO CUSTODY
OF DEPARTMENT OF CORRECTIONS

THE CIRCUIT COURT OF CALUSA COUNTY, IN THE SPRING TERM of 20XX-8
IN THE CASE OF:

STATE OF XXXXXX

v. CASE ID : 20XX(-8)1492 DIVISION: D

DEFENDANT : Chris Alexander
AKA(S) : Frostie

IN THE NAME AND BY AUTHORITY OF THE STATE OF XXXXX, TO THE SHERRIFF OF SAID COUNTY AND THE DEPARTMENT OF CORRECTIONS OF SAID STATE, GREETING:

THE ABOVE NAMED DEFENDANT HAVING BEEN DULY CHARGED WITH THE OFFENSE SPECIFIED HEREIN IN THE ABOVE STYLED COURT, AND HAVING BEEN DULY CONVICTED AND ADJUDICATED GUILTY OF AND SENTENCE FOR SAID OFFENSE BY SAID COURT, AS APPEARS FROM THE ATTACHED CERTIFIED COPIES OF INFORMATION FILED JUDGMENT AND SENTENCE, AND FELONY DISPOSITION AND SENTENCE DATA FROM WHICH ARE HEREBY MADE PARTS HEREOF;

NOW THEREFORE, THIS TO COMMAND YOU, THE SAID SHERIFF, TO TAKE AND KEEP, AND, WITHIN A REASONABLE TIME AFTER RECEIVING THIS COMMITMENT, SAFELY DELIVER THE SAID DEFENDANT, TOGETHER WITH ANY PERTINENT INVESTIGATION REPORT PREPARED IN THIS CASE, INTO THE CUSTODY OF THE DEPARTMENT OF CORRECTIONS OF THE STATE OF XXXXX: AND THIS IS TO COMMAND YOU, THE SAID DEPARTMENT OF CORRECTIONS, BY AND THROUGH YOUR SECRETARY, REGIONAL DIRECTORS, SUPERINTENDANTS, AND OTHER OFFICIALS, TO KEEP AND SAFELY IMPRISON THE SAID DEFENDANT FRO THE TERM OF SAID SENTENCE IN THE INSTITUTION IN THE STATE CORRECTIONAL SYSTEM TO WHICH YOU, THE SAID DEPARTMENT OF CORRECTIONS, MAY CAUSE THE SAID DEFENDANT TO BE CONVEYED OR THEREAFTER TRANSFERRED. AND THESE PRESENTS SHALL BE YOUR AUTHORITY FOR THE SAME. HEREIN NOT FAIL.

WITNESS THE HONORABLE JEREMY PARKER
JUDGE OF THE SAID COURT, AS ALSO CONNIE EVANS
CLERK, AND THE SEAL THEREOF, THIS
24th DAY OF May 20XX-8

BY: *Margaret Mills*
DEPUTY CLERK

IN THE FIRST JUDICIAL CIRCUIT IN AND FOR
CALUSA COUNTY, STATE OF XXXXX

CIRCUIT CRIMINAL DIVISON

STATE OF XXXXX v. <u>CHRIS ALEXANDER</u> DEFENDANT	DIVISION: D CASE NUMBER: 20XX(-8)1492

CERTIFICATE OF SERVICE

I, Connie Evans, Clerk of the Circuit Court of the County of Calusa, State of XXXXX, having by law the custody of the seal and all records, books, documents and papers of or appertaining to the Circuit Court, do hereby certify that a true and correct copy of the Judgment and Sentence has been hand delivered to the State Attorney and mailed to the Defense Attorney.

IN WITNESS WHEREOF, I have hereunto set my hand and seal of said Circuit Court, this 24th day of May A.D. 20XX-8.

CONNIE EVANS
As Clerk of Circuit Court

Margaret Mills
As Deputy Clerk
Circuit Criminal Division

IN THE CIRCUIT COURT, 1ST JUDICIAL CIRCUIT
IN AND FOR CALUSA COUNTY, XXXXX
DIVISION : D
CASE NUMBER : 20XX(-8)1492

STATE OF XXXXX
v.
Chris Alexander
DEFENDANT

---JUDGMENT---

THE DEFENDANT, Chris Alexander, BEING PERSONALLY BEFORE
THIS COURT REPRESENTED WITH
PRIVATE ATTORNEY
Norm Pearson, Esquire
THE ATTORNEY OF RECORD AND THE STATE REPRESENTED BY ASSISTANT STATE ATTORNEY
George Peabody Smalley, AND HAVING

Been tried and found guilty by a jury of the following crime(s): 1

COUNT	CRIME	STATUTE	COURT ACTION	DATE
1	Possession of a Controlled Substance, to wit, MARIJUANA	80112	GUILTY	16 April 20XX-8
2	Sale of a Controlled Substance, to wit, Marijuana	80112a	GUILTY	16 April 20XX-8

And no cause being shown why the defendant should not be adjudicated guilty, it is ordered that the defendant is hereby adjudicated guilty of the above crime(s).

DEFENDANT Chris Alexander

Division : D
Case Number : 20XX(-8)1492
OBTS Number : 98421119

SENTENCE

THE DEFENDANT, BEING PERSONALLY BEFORE THIS COURT, ACCOMPANIED BY THE DEFENDANT'S ATTORNEY OF RECORD, PRIVATE ATTORNEY Norm Pearson, Esquire AND HAVING BEEN ADJUDGED GUILTY HEREIN, AND THE COURT HAVING BEEN GIVEN THE DEFENDANT AN OPPORTUNITY TO BE HEARD AND TO OFFER MATTERS IN MITIGATION OF SENTENCE, AND TO SHOW CAUSE WHY THE DEFENDANT SHOULD NOT BE SENTENCED AS PROVIDED BY LAW AND NO CAUSE BEING SHOWN

IT IS THE SENTENCE OF THIS COURT THAT THE DEFENDANT:

Pay a fine of $2500.00, pursuant to appropriate XXXXX Statutes.

Is hereby committed to the custody of the Department of Corrections for a term of: 4 Years, sentence to be suspended pending successful completion of 4 years probation.

OTHER PROVISIONS

AS TO COUNT(S) : 1
THE FOLLOWING MANDATORY/MINIMUM PROVISIONS APPLY TO THE SENTENCE IMPOSED :

DEFENDANT Chris Alexander

Division : D
Case Number : 20XX(-8)1492
OBTS Number : 98421119

OTHER PROVISIONS

Sentencing guidelines filed.

IN THE EVENT THE ABOVE SENTENCE IS TO THE DEPARTMENT OF CORRECTIONS, THE SHERIFF OF CALUSA COUNTY, XXXXX, IS HEREBY ORDERED AND DIRECTED TO DELIVER THE DEFENDANT TO THE DEPARTMENT OF CORRECTIONS AT THE FACILITY DESIGNATED BY THE DEPARTMENT TOGETHER WITH A COPY OF THIS JUDGMENT AND SENTENCE AND ANY OTHER DOCUMENTS SPECIFIED BY XXXXX STATUTE
THE DEFENDANT IN OPEN COURT WAS ADVISED OF THE RIGHT TO APPEAL FROM THIS SENTENCE BY FILING NOTICE OF APPEAL WITHIN 30 DAYS FROM THIS DATE WITH THE CLERK OF THIS COURT AND THE DEFENDANT'S RIGHT TO THE ASSISTANCE OF COUNSEL IN TAKING THE APPEAL AT THE EXPENSE OF THE STATE SHOWING OF INDIGENCY.

DONE AND ORDERED IN CALUSA COUNTY, XXXXX, THIS 24TH DAY OF May 20XX-8

State of XXXXX
UNIFORM COMMITMENT TO CUSTODY
OF DEPARTMENT OF CORRECTIONS

THE CIRCUIT COURT OF CALUSA COUNTY, IN THE SPRING TERM of 20XX-8
IN THE CASE OF:

STATE OF XXXXX CASE ID : 20XX(-3)1898 DIVISION: D
v.
DEFENDANT : Nikki Long
AKA(S) :

IN THE NAME AND BY AUTHORITY OF THE STATE OF XXXXX, TO THE SHERIFF OF SAID COUNTY AND THE DEPARTMENT OF CORRECTIONS OF SAID STATE, GREETING:

THE ABOVE NAMED DEFENDANT HAVING BEEN DULY CHARGED WITH THE OFFENSE SPECIFIED HEREIN IN THE ABOVE STYLED COURT, AND HAVING BEEN DULY CONVICTED AND ADJUDICATED GUILTY OF AND SENTENCE FOR SAID OFFENSE BY SAID COURT, AS APPEARS FROM THE ATTACHED CERTIFIED COPIES OF INFORMATION FILED JUDGMENT AND SENTENCE, AND FELONY DISPOSITION AND SENTENCE DATA FROM WHICH ARE HEREBY MADE PARTS HEREOF;

NOW THEREFORE, THIS TO COMMAND YOU, THE SAID SHERIFF, TO TAKE AND KEEP, AND, WITHIN A REASONABLE TIME AFTER RECEIVING THIS COMMITMENT, SAFELY DELIVER THE SAID DEFENDANT, TOGETHER WITH ANY PERTINENT INVESTIGATION REPORT PREPARED IN THIS CASE, INTO THE CUSTODY OF THE DEPARTMENT OF CORRECTIONS OF THE STATE OF XXXXX: AND THIS IS TO COMMAND YOU, THE SAID DEPARTMENT OF CORRECTIONS, BY AND THROUGH YOUR SECRETARY, REGIONAL DIRECTORS, SUPERINTENDANTS, AND OTHER OFFICIALS, TO KEEP AND SAFELY IMPRISON THE SAID DEFENDANT FRO THE TERM OF SAID SENTENCE IN THE INSTITUTION IN THE STATE CORRECTIONAL SYSTEM TO WHICH YOU, THE SAID DEPARTMENT OF CORRECTIONS, MAY CAUSE THE SAID DEFENDANT TO BE CONVEYED OR THEREAFTER TRANSFERRED. AND THESE PRESENTS SHALL BE YOUR AUTHORITY FOR THE SAME. HEREIN NOT FAIL.

WITNESS THE HONORABLE JEREMY PARKER
JUDGE OF THE SAID COURT, AS ALSO CONNIE EVANS
CLERK, AND THE SEAL THEREOF, THIS
21st DAY OF January 20XX-3

BY: MARGARET MILLS
DEPUTY CLERK

IN THE FIRST JUDICIAL CIRCUIT IN AND FOR
CALUSA COUNTY, STATE OF XXXXX

CIRCUIT CRIMINAL DIVISON

STATE OF XXXXX
V.
Nikki Long
DEFENDANT

DIVISION: D

CASE NUMBER: 20XX(-1)1898

CERTIFICATE OF SERVICE

I, Connie Evans, Clerk of the Circuit Court of the County of Calusa, State of XXXXX, having by law the custody of the seal and all records, books, documents and papers of or appertaining to the Circuit Court, do hereby certify that a true and correct copy of the Judgment and Sentence has been hand delivered to the State Attorney and mailed to the Defense Attorney.

IN WITNESS WHEREOF, I have hereunto set my hand and seal of said Circuit Court, this 21st day of January A.D. 20XX-3.

CONNIE EVANS
As Clerk of Circuit Court

MARGARET MILLS
As Deputy Clerk
Circuit Criminal Division

IN THE CIRCUIT COURT, 1ST JUDICIAL CIRCUIT
IN AND FOR CALUSA COUNTY, XXXXX
DIVISION : D
CASE NUMBER : 20XX(-3)1898

STATE OF XXXXX
VS
Nikki Long
DEFENDANT

---JUDGMENT---

THE DEFENDANT, Nikki Long, BEING PERSONALLY BEFORE THIS COURT REPRESENTED WITH PRIVATE ATTORNEY
Norm Pearson, Esquire
THE ATTORNEY OF RECORD AND THE STATE REPRESENTED BY ASSISTANT STATE ATTORNEY
George Peabody Smalley, AND HAVING

Been tried and found guilty by a jury of the following crime(s): 1

COUNT	CRIME	STATUTE	COURT ACTION	DATE
1	Filing a false police report	80107	GUILTY	14 Dec 20XX-4

And no cause being shown why the defendant should not be adjudicated guilty, it is ordered that the defendant is hereby adjudicated guilty of the above crime(s).

DEFENDANT Nikki Long

Division	:	D
Case Number	:	20XX(-3)1898
OBTS Number	:	32323498

-------SENTENCE-------

THE DEFENDANT, BEING PERSONALLY BEFORE THIS COURT, ACCOMPANIED BY THE DEFENDANT'S ATTORNEY OF RECORD, PRIVATE ATTORNEY Norm Pearson, Esquire

AND HAVING BEEN ADJUDGED GUILTY HEREIN, AND THE COURT HAVING BEEN GIVEN THE DEFENDANT AN OPPORTUNITY TO BE HEARD AND TO OFFER MATTERS IN MITIGATION OF SENTENCE, AND TO SHOW CAUSE WHY THE DEFENDANT SHOULD NOT BE SENTENCED AS PROVIDED BY LAW AND NO CAUSE BEING SHOWN

IT IS THE SENTENCE OF THIS COURT THAT THE DEFENDANT:

Pay a fine of $750.00, pursuant to appropriate XXXXX Statutes. Is hereby committed to the custody of the Department of Corrections for a term of: 18 Months, sentence to be suspended pending successful completion of 2 years probation.

-------OTHER PROVISIONS-------

AS TO COUNT(S): 1
THE FOLLOWING MANDATORY/MINIMUM PROVISIONS APPLY TO THE SENTENCE IMPOSED:

None

DEFENDANT Nikki Long

Division	:	D
Case Number	:	20XX(-3)1898
OBTS Number	:	32323498

-------OTHER PROVISIONS-------

Sentencing guidelines filed.

IN THE EVENT THE ABOVE SENTENCE IS TO THE DEPARTMENT OF CORRECTIONS, THE SHERIFF OF CALUSA COUNTY, XXXXX, IS HEREBY ORDERED AND DIRECTED TO DELIVER THE DEFENDANT TO THE DEPARTMENT OF CORRECTIONS AT THE FACILITY DESIGNATED BY THE DEPARTMENT TOGETHER WITH A COPY OF THIS JUDGMENT AND SENTENCE AND ANY OTHER DOCUMENTS SPECIFIED BY XXXXX STATUTE

THE DEFENDANT IN OPEN COURT WAS ADVISED OF THE RIGHT TO APPEAL FROM THIS SENTENCE BY FILING NOTICE OF APPEAL WITHIN 30 DAYS FROM THIS DATE WITH THE CLERK OF THIS COURT AND THE DEFENDANT'S RIGHT TO THE ASSISTANCE OF COUNSEL IN TAKING THE APPEAL AT THE EXPENSE OF THE STATE SHOWING OF INDIGENCY.

DONE AND ORDERED IN CALUSA COUNTY, XXXXX, THIS 21st DAY OF January 20XX-3

State of XXXXX
UNIFORM COMMITMENT TO CUSTODY
OF DEPARTMENT OF CORRECTIONS

THE CIRCUIT COURT OF CALUSA COUNTY, IN THE SPRING TERM of 20XX-8
IN THE CASE OF:

STATE OF XXXXX CASE ID : 20XX(-6)1066 DIVISION: D
v.
DEFENDANT : Nikki Long
AKA(S) :

IN THE NAME AND BY AUTHORITY OF THE STATE OF XXXXX, TO THE SHERRIFF OF SAID COUNTY AND THE DEPARTMENT OF CORRECTIONS OF SAID STATE, GREETING:

THE ABOVE NAMED DEFENDANT HAVING BEEN DULY CHARGED WITH THE OFFENSE SPECIFIED HEREIN IN THE ABOVE STYLED COURT, AND HAVING BEEN DULY CONVICTED AND ADJUDICATED GUILTY OF AND SENTENCE FOR SAID OFFENSE BY SAID COURT, AS APPEARS FROM THE ATTACHED CERTIFIED COPIES OF INFORMATION FILED JUDGMENT AND SENTENCE, AND FELONY DISPOSITION AND SENTENCE DATA FROM WHICH ARE HEREBY MADE PARTS HEROF;

NOW THEREFORE, THIS TO COMMAND YOU, THE SAID SHERIFF, TO TAKE AND KEEP, AND, WITHIN A REASONABLE TIME AFTER RECEIVING THIS COMMITMENT, SAFELY DELIVER THE SAID DEFENDANT, TOGETHER WITH ANY PERTINENT INVESTIGATION REPORT PREPARED IN THIS CASE, INTO THE CUSTODY OF THE DEPARTMENT OF CORRECTIONS OF THE STATE OF XXXXX: AND THIS IS TO COMMAND YOU, THE SAID DEPARTMENT OF CORRECTIONS, BY AND THROUGH YOUR SECRETARY, REGIONAL DIRECTORS, SUPERINTENDANTS, AND OTHER OFFICIALS, TO KEEP AND SAFELY IMPRISON THE SAID DEFENDANT FRO THE TERM OF SAID SENTENCE IN THE INSTITUTION IN THE STATE CORRECTIONAL SYSTEM TO WHICH YOU, THE SAID DEPARTMENT OF CORRECTIONS, MAY CAUSE THE SAID DEFENDANT TO BE CONVEYED OR THEREAFTER TRANSFERRED. AND THESE PRESENTS SHALL BE YOUR AUTHORITY FOR THE SAME. HEREIN NOT FAIL.

WITNESS THE HONORABLE JEREMY PARKER
JUDGE OF THE SAID COURT, AS ALSO CONNIE EVANS
CLERK, AND THE SEAL THEREOF, THIS
24th DAY OF February 20XX-6

BY: MARGARET MILLS
DEPUTY CLERK

IN THE FIRST JUDICIAL CIRCUIT IN AND FOR
CALUSA COUNTY, STATE OF XXXXX

CIRCUIT CRIMINAL DIVISON

STATE OF XXXXX
v.
Nikki Long
DEFENDANT

DIVISION: D

CASE NUMBER: 20XX(-6)1066

CERTIFICATE OF SERVICE

I, Connie Evans, Clerk of the Circuit Court of the County of Calusa, State of XXXXX, having by law the custody of the seal and all records, books, documents and papers of or appertaining to the Circuit Court, do hereby certify that a true and correct copy of the Judgment and Sentence has been hand delivered to the State Attorney and mailed to the Defense Attorney.

IN WITNESS WHEREOF, I have hereunto set my hand and seal of said Circuit Court, this 24th day of February A.D. 20XX-6.

CONNIE EVANS
As Clerk of Circuit Court

MARGARET MILLS
As Deputy Clerk
Circuit Criminal Division

IN THE CIRCUIT COURT, 1ST JUDICIAL CIRCUIT
IN AND FOR CALUSA COUNTY, XXXXX
DIVISION : D
CASE NUMBER : 20XX(-6)1066

STATE OF XXXXX
VS
Nikki Long
DEFENDANT

--JUDGMENT--

THE DEFENDANT, Nikki Long, BEING PERSONALLY BEFORE THIS COURT REPRESENTED WITH PRIVATE ATTORNEY
Norm Pearson, Esquire
THE ATTORNEY OF RECORD AND THE STATE REPRESENTED BY ASSISTANT STATE ATTORNEY
George Peabody Smalley, AND HAVING

Been tried and found guilty by a jury of the following crime(s): 1

COUNT	CRIME	STATUTE	COURT ACTION	DATE
1	Possession of a Controlled Substance, to wit, MARIJUANA	80112	GUILTY	9 January 20XX-6

And no cause being shown why the defendant should not be adjudicated guilty, it is ordered that the defendant is hereby adjudicated guilty of the above crime(s).

DEFENDANT Nikki Long

Division	:	D
Case Number	:	20XX(-6)1066
OBTS Number	:	32323498

------SENTENCE------

THE DEFENDANT, BEING PERSONALLY BEFORE THIS COURT, ACCOMPANIED BY THE DEFENDANT'S ATTORNEY OF RECORD, PRIVATE ATTORNEY Norm Pearson, Esquire

AND HAVING BEEN ADJUDGED GUILTY HEREIN, AND THE COURT HAVING BEEN GIVEN THE DEFENDANT AN OPPORTUNITY TO BE HEARD AND TO OFFER MATTERS IN MITIGATION OF SENTENCE, AND TO SHOW CAUSE WHY THE DEFENDANT SHOULD NOT BE SENTENCED AS PROVIDED BY LAW AND NO CAUSE BEING SHOWN

IT IS THE SENTENCE OF THIS COURT THAT THE DEFENDANT:

Pay a fine of $500.00, pursuant to appropriate XXXXX Statutes. Is hereby committed to the custody of the Department of Corrections for a term of: 1 Year, sentence to be suspended pending successful completion of 2 years probation.

------OTHER PROVISIONS------

AS TO COUNT(S) : 1

THE FOLLOWING MANDATORY/MINIMUM PROVISIONS APPLY TO THE SENTENCE IMPOSED :

None

DEFENDANT Nikki Long

Division	:	D
Case Number	:	20XX(-6)1066
OBTS Number	:	32323498

------OTHER PROVISIONS------

Sentencing guidelines filed.

IN THE EVENT THE ABOVE SENTENCE IS TO THE DEPARTMENT OF CORRECTIONS, THE SHERIFF OF CALUSA COUNTY, XXXXX, IS HEREBY ORDERED AND DIRECTED TO DELIVER THE DEFENDANT TO THE DEPARTMENT OF CORRECTIONS AT THE FACILITY DESIGNATED BY THE DEPARTMENT TOGETHER WITH A COPY OF THIS JUDGMENT AND SENTENCE AND ANY OTHER DOCUMENTS SPECIFIED BY XXXXX STATUTE

THE DEFENDANT IN OPEN COURT WAS ADVISED OF THE RIGHT TO APPEAL FROM THIS SENTENCE BY FILING NOTICE OF APPEAL WITHIN 30 DAYS FROM THIS DATE WITH THE CLERK OF THIS COURT AND THE DEFENDANT'S RIGHT TO THE ASSISTANCE OF COUNSEL IN TAKING THE APPEAL AT THE EXPENSE OF THE STATE SHOWING OF INDIGENCY.

DONE AND ORDERED IN CALUSA COUNTY, XXXXX, THIS 24TH DAY OF February 20XX-6

Fundamental Trial Advocacy:
The Law, the Skill & the Art

Washington v. Hartwell

Cases and Materials

Charles H. Rose, III
Professor of Excellence in Trial Advocacy
Director, Center for Excellence in Advocacy
Stetson University College of Law

Notes

WASHINGTON V. HARTWELL

CHARLES H. ROSE III
Associate Professor of Law
Director, Center for Excellence in Advocacy
Stetson University College of Law

"We empower students to find within themselves their unique voices – to become the best possible advocates they can be."[1]

The following student at Stetson University College of Law gave of their time, expertise and creativity to assist in producing this case file. Without their help this project would still be an idea that was less than half way to completion. Each embodies the Stetson Spirit and I gratefully acknowledge their contributions. They are:

Center for Excellence in Advocacy Fellows-
Vilma Martinez
Allana Forté
Katherine Lambrose

Case File Project Volunteers-
Derrick Connell
Nadine David
Brian Dettman
Natasha Hines
Lindsay Moczynski

I wish to express my gratitude to the leadership at Stetson - Dean Darby Dickerson, Associate Dean Ellen Podgor, and Associate Dean Jamie Fox. They helped make this text possible through their unfailing support of creative scholarship.

The ideas behind using case files to teach are grounded in concepts of experiential learning. It is in doing that true education occurs.[2] These files are designed to create optimal "learning by doing" opportunities – the foundation upon which advocacy instruction, if not all learning, rests.

---

[1] Professor Charles H. Rose III, Director, Center for Excellence in Advocacy, www.law.stetson.edu/excellence/advocacy

[2] Myles Horton, the co-founder of the Highlander Folk School, referred to this with a phrase from a Spanish song that translated reads "We make the road by walking." One of the best captured thoughts about experiential learning I have ever read.

– Introduction –

These case files are scalable, adaptable, and relevant to the issues facing 21st century advocates. They are based on the lessons learned by Stetson's faculty, students and alumni, reflecting the same commitment to excellence embodied in our Law School's award winning advocacy teams and national reputation in Advocacy.

A commitment to the law, the skill and the art of advocacy creates persuasive advocacy. The foundation begins with the ***process***: it's the way we train, the way we learn, and the way we practice. This is experiential learning. These case files focus the advocates on specific advocacy skills in a simulated real world environment, allowing participants to learn the skill and the law in the context of a moment in the trial. The exercises accompanying the case file develop advocacy ***skills*** through the rubric of the experiential learning process. This approach allows the advocate to develop ***values*** that contextually reflect the legal profession. These case files provide a structure for the ***process, skills*** and ***values*** involved in becoming a better advocate.

The goal of this effort is to design a well-crafted, challenging case file that promotes excellence in all facets of advocacy instruction. The way in which a case file is organized, presented and supported is a balancing act that either increases or decreases its effectiveness. The result of this balancing act is a unique, multi-media product that provides both academics and the practicing bar with modular course content producing varied levels of difficulty (novice, intermediate, and advanced), that is developed for, and measured by, quantifiable outcome assessments.

Washington v. Hartwell

CASE FILE CONTENTS

Tab A: Introduction..........1

- Introduction to the Case
- Jury Instructions
- Verdict Form

Tab B: Court Filings..........13

- Summons
- Complaint
- Answer and Affirmative Defenses
- Request for Documents
- Interrogatory

Tab C: Police Investigations..........35

- Report of Incident – James Record
- Report of Investigation – Edwin Morris
    - 911 Call transcript
    - Photos of area
    - Diagrams of area
    - Photos of Oldest Decedent
    - Sun Up and Sun Down Report
    - Statement of Johnny Broadsides
    - Statement of Dimitri Merinov
    - Statement of Bill Hartwell
    - Statement of Marian Hartwell
    - Statement of Matt Bader
    - Video 1 of fleeing vehicle

- Video 2 of fleeing vehicle
- 9-1-1 call .mp3 file
- Affidavit of Lieutenant James Allen Record

Tab D: Newspaper Articles..........71

- Calusa County Courier Article
- Pelican Bay Star - Letter to the Editor

Tab E: Statements of the Parties..........73

- Statement of Charissa Washington
- Statement of Rebecca Hartwell

Tab F: Conviction Reports..........79

- Dimitri Merinov Record of Conviction for Exhibition
- Matt Bader Record of Conviction for Cocaine Possession
- Rebecca Hartwell Record of Conviction for Reckless Driving
- Charissa Washington Record of Convictions for Filing a False Police Report and Possession of Marijuana

Washington v. Hartwell

INTRODUCTION

The children were black. The driver was white. The community was outraged. It was a media circus. Was it one vehicle, two or three? A van? A dark blue Honda? A Toyota? Or was it all three? The witnesses couldn't agree. The car sped away as a horrified crowd of about 200 emptied into the street and began shouting in outrage. Children's shoes and sandals were scattered on the pavement. Next to a puddle of blood was a pillow left behind by paramedics who had treated one of the victims. Were the non-working streetlights also to blame? Did someone hide the car? Was DNA removed from the evidence? What were the unsupervised children doing in a high-traffic area at night? Who would pay? After being sought for days, a high-profile criminal defense attorney, Steve Levine, finally announced that the driver would come forward.

On March 21, 20XX-2 at approximately 7:15 p.m., Ms. Rebecca Hartwell was driving her midnight blue Toyota Echo. She was travelling north on 39th Street. It is undisputed that at some point her car hit at least two of the four children crossing the street. She also fled the scene of the accident. The hit-and-run crash killed two brothers, aged 14 and 3, and seriously injured a 2-year-old boy and a 7-year-old girl. The 3 year old boy was caught underneath the grill of Ms. Hartwell's car and dragged approximately 150 feet before his body worked its way loose and came to final rest in the middle of 39th Street. The Toyota then fled the scene of the accident.

The criminal case has ended. Judge Jerry Parker oversaw the prosecution for negligent homicide that resulted in a hung jury on July 13, 20XX-1. The prosecution's office has indicated that they have no intention of retrying the case, citing evidentiary concerns and proof difficulties. Steve Levine contends that the nature of this trial caused the hung jury to have the effect of a dismissal with prejudice. The state's office has publically stated that they disagree with that assessment.

A civil case has been filed alleging both wrongful death and defamation. After filing answers and affirmative defenses to the Complaint, civil defense counsel moved for a change of venue. The Motion was denied.

LOCAL RULES: Calusa County follows the **Federal Rules of Civil Procedure** and has adopted the **Federal Rules of Evidence**. There are some local evidentiary and statutory distinctions litigants must consider. Those relevant Calusa County-specific rules and law have been provided in the law section of this case file.

PRELIMINARY JURY INSTRUCTIONS

You have now been sworn as the jury to try this case. This is a civil case involving a disputed claim or claims between the parties. Those claims and other matters will be explained to you later. By your verdict, you will decide the disputed issues of fact. I will decide the questions of law that arise during the trial, and before you retire to deliberate at the close of the trial, I will instruct you on the law that you are to follow and apply in reaching your verdict. It is your responsibility to determine the facts and to apply the law to those facts. Thus, the function of the jury and the function of the judge are well defined, and they do not overlap. This is one of the fundamental principles of our system of justice.

Before proceeding further, it will be helpful for you to understand how a trial is conducted. In a few moments, the attorneys for the parties will have an opportunity to make opening statements, in which they may explain to you the, issues in the case and summarize the facts that they expect the evidence will show. Following the opening statements, witnesses will be called to testify under oath. They will be examined and cross-examined by the attorneys. Documents and other exhibits also may be received as evidence.

After all the evidence has been received, the attorneys will again have the opportunity to address you and to make their final arguments. The statements that the attorneys now make and the arguments that they later make are not to be considered by you either as evidence in the case or as your instruction on the law. Nevertheless, these statements and arguments are intended to help you properly understand the issues, the evidence, and the applicable law, so you should give them your close attention. Following the final arguments by the attorneys, I will instruct you on the law.

You should give careful attention to the testimony and other evidence as it is received and presented for your consideration, but you should not form or express any opinion about the case until you have received all the evidence, the arguments of the attorneys, and the instructions on the law from me. In other words, you should not form or express any opinion about the case until you retire to the jury room to consider you verdict

The attorneys are trained in the rules of evidence and trial procedure, and it is their duty to make all objections they feel are proper. When a lawyer makes an objection, I will either overrule or sustain the objection. If I overrule an objection to a question, the witness will answer the question. If I sustain an objection, the witness will not answer, but you must not, speculate on what might have happened or what the witness might have said had I permitted the witness to answer the question. You should not draw any inference from the question itself.

During the trial, it may be necessary for me to confer with the attorneys out of your hearing, talking about matters of law and other matters that require consideration by me alone. It is impossible for me to predict when such a conference may be required or how long it will last. When such conferences occur, they will be conducted so as to consume as little of your time as necessary for a fair and orderly trial of the case.

At this time, the attorneys for the parties will have an opportunity to make their opening statements, in which they may explain to you the issues in this case and give you a summary of the facts they expect the evidence will show.

FINAL JURY INSTRUCTIONS

Members of the jury, I shall now instruct you on the law that you must follow in reaching your verdict. It is your duty as jurors to decide the issues, and only those issues, that I submit for determination by your verdict. In reaching your verdict, you should consider and weigh the evidence, decide the disputed issues of fact and apply the law on which I shall instruct you to the facts as you find them from the evidence.

The evidence in this case consists of the sworn testimony of the witnesses, all exhibits received into evidence, and all facts that may be admitted or agreed to by the parties. In determining the facts, you may draw reasonable inferences from the evidence. You may make deductions and reach conclusions which reason and common sense lead you to draw from the facts shown by the evidence in this case, but you should not speculate on any matters outside the evidence.

In determining the believability of any witness and the weight to be given the testimony of any witness, you may properly consider the demeanor of the witness while testifying; the frankness or lack of frankness of the witness; the intelligence of the witness; any interest the witness may have in the outcome of the case; the means and opportunity the, witness had to know the facts about which the witness testified; the ability of the witness to remember the matters about which the witness testified; and the reasonableness of the testimony of the witness, considered in the light of all the evidence in the case and in light of your own experience and common sense.

The issues for your determination on the wrongful death claim of Charissa Washington against Rebecca Hartwell is whether Rebecca Hartwell was negligent when she struck Ronald and Jordan Washington with the vehicle she operated on the evening of March 21, 20XX, and, if so, whether such negligence was a legal cause of the loss, injury, or damage suffered by Charissa Washington and/or the Estates Jordan and Ronald Washington.

"Negligence" is the failure to use reasonable care. Reasonable care is that degree of care which a reasonably careful person would use under like circumstances. Negligence may consist either of doing something that a reasonably careful person would not do under like circumstances or failing to do something that a reasonably careful person would do under like circumstances.

Negligence is a legal cause of loss, injury, or damage if it directly and in natural and continuous sequence produces or contributes substantially to producing such loss, injury, or damages that it can reasonably be said that but for the negligence the loss, injury, or damage would not have occurred.

If the greater weight of the evidence does not support the claim of Charissa Washington and/or the Estate, then your verdict should be for Rebecca Hartwell. "Greater weight of the evidence" means the more persuasive and convincing force and effect of the entire evidence in this case. However, if the greater weight of the evidence supports either Charissa Washington's individual claims or the Estate's claim, then you should consider the defenses raised by Rebecca Hartwell.

Rebecca Hartwell has raised a defense in this case which permits you, the jury, to determine whether persons who are not parties to this lawsuit may have also contributed to the injuries of the Washington's and/or the Estate. If you find that Rebecca Hartwell was negligent in her operation of her motor vehicle and that her negligence caused or contributed to the Washington's injury and/or the Estate's injury, you should determine what percentage of the total fault is chargeable to Rebecca Hartwell.

If you find that Ronald and Jordan Washington were negligent in their decision to cross the street and that their negligence caused or contributed to the injuries and/or the Estate's injury, you should determine what percentage of the total fault is chargeable to Ronald and Jordan Washington. In determining whether Ronald and Jordan Washington were negligent, you must consider whether they exercised reasonable care for their own safety. Reasonable care on the part of a child is that degree of care which a reasonably careful child of the same age, mental capacity, intelligence, training and experience would use under like circumstances.

At this point in the trial, you, as jurors, are deciding only if Rebecca Hartwell was negligent, and if Ronald and Jordan Washington were negligent. You will first return a verdict on that issue.

Additionally, the plaintiff, Charissa Washington, claims that the defendant, Rebecca Hartwell, defamed her when she made statements about the quality of Ms. Washington's parenting of the children on the day of the accident. These statements were allegedly made by Ms. Hartwell and published in the Pelican Daily Star.

In order to recover under her defamation claim(s), Charissa Washington must prove the following: that Rebecca Hartwell made the alleged statement(s); Rebecca Hartwell made the defamatory statement(s) with malice toward the Charissa Washington or with a reckless disregard for her interests; the defendant published the defamatory statement(s) to a person other than the defendant; the plaintiff was damaged; and the Plaintiff's damages were caused by the Rebecca Hartwell's defamatory statement(s).

A person acts with malice if she makes a false statement with knowledge of its falsity, or if she makes it for the specific purpose of injuring another person. A person acts with reckless disregard if she consciously disregards and is indifferent to the truth or falsity of the statement. It is not necessary for Charissa Washington to prove that Rebecca Hartwell deliberately intended to injure her. It is sufficient if Rebecca Hartwell acted with reckless disregard for the truth or falsity of her statements.

In determining whether Rebecca Hartwell acted with malice or reckless disregard, you may consider the following factors: a) did Rebecca Hartwell reasonably rely on the circumstances known to him when he made the statements; b) did the Rebecca Hartwell make the statement in good faith and believing it to be true; c) did the Defendant act with spite or ill will toward Charissa Washington; did she intend to injure her reputation, good name or feelings;

d) did Rebecca Hartwell attempt to minimize any harm to Charissa Washington by apologizing or retracting a statement within a reasonable time after determining a statement to be false?

Substantial truth is a defense to defamation. Substantially true means that the substance or gist of the statement is true. If the defendant proves that a statement was substantially true, then your verdict must be for the defendant with regard to that statement.

Qualified privilege is also a defense to a defamation claim. This jurisdiction recognizes a qualified privilege for statements made within certain business and social relationships. The privilege is qualified because it is not an absolute defense.

Burdens of Proof:

Charissa Washington has the burden of proving her claim of defamation, namely, that Rebecca Hartwell made a statement that defamed her; that it was communicated to another person; that she was injured by the defamatory statement; and that the Rebecca Hartwell made the statement with malice or reckless disregard. If you find that the Charissa Washington has proven each of these elements, then your verdict must be for the Charissa Washington, unless you find that the statement is true.

Rebecca Hartwell has the burden of proving the defense of truth. If you find that a statement was true, then your verdict must be for Rebecca Hartwell with regard to that statement.

Damages:

If you find for Charissa Washington on any of her claims for wrongful death/negligence and/or defamation, then you shall determine her damages in an amount that will justly and fairly compensate her for the harm caused by Rebecca Hartwell's defamatory statement or statements. In determining damages you may consider the injury to Charissa Washington's reputation and good name, any physical or mental suffering she may have sustained, and any loss of earnings or harm to business and employment relations. You may also, in your discretion, assess punitive damages against Rebecca Hartwell as punishment and as a deterrent to others. If you find that punitive damages should be assessed against Rebecca Hartwell, you may consider the financial resources of Rebecca Hartwell in fixing the amount. Punitive damages are awarded to punish the Defendant, not to compensate the Plaintiff.

Your verdict must be based on the evidence that has been received and the law on which I have instructed you. In reaching your verdict, you are not to be swayed from the performance of your duty by prejudice, sympathy, or any other sentiment for or against any party.

When you retire to the jury room, you should select one of your members to act as foreperson, to preside over your deliberations, and to sign your verdict. Your verdict must be unanimous; that is, your verdict must be agreed to by each of you. You will be given a verdict form, which I shall now read and, explain to you.

(READ VERDICT FORM)

When you have agreed on your verdict, the foreperson, acting for the jury, should date and sign the verdict form and return it to the courtroom. You may now retire to consider your verdict.

IN THE CIRCUIT COURT OF FIRST JUDICIAL DISTICT
CALUSA COUNTY, XXXXX
CIVIL DIVISION

CHARISSA WASHINGTON,)
Plaintiff,)
) CASE NO.: 20XX-1439
v.)
) DIVISION: A
)
REBECCA HARTWELL,)
Defendant.)

JURY VERDICT

The jury must answer the following interrogatories. The foreperson is to answer the interrogatories for the jury and sign the verdict.

Interrogatory No. 1: Did Rebecca Hartwell fail to exercise reasonable care during the March 21, 20XX-2 incident?

YES _____
NO _____

Interrogatory No. 2: If the answer to No. 1 is *YES*, was Rebecca Hartwell's negligence the direct cause of damage to Charissa Washington?

YES _____
NO _____

Interrogatory No. 3: If the answer to No. 1 is *YES*, did Charissa Washington contribute in any way to the cause of her damage?

YES _____
NO _____

Interrogatory No. 4: Please determine the amount of damages necessary to justly and fairly compensate the Plaintiff:

Amount $ __________

Interrogatory No. 5: Did Defendant make a defamatory statement about the Plaintiff?

YES _____
NO _____

Interrogatory No. 6: Did Defendant make the defamatory statement with malice toward the Plaintiff, or with a reckless disregard for her interests?

YES _____
NO _____

Interrogatory No. 7: Did Defendant publish the defamatory statement to a person other than the Plaintiff?

YES _____
NO _____

Interrogatory No. 8: Was the defamatory statement true?

YES _____
NO _____

Interrogatory No. 9: Was the defamatory statement made on a subject in which the Defendant had an important interest or duty--either legal, moral, business, or social--and made to another person having a like interest or duty?

YES _____
NO _____

Interrogatory No. 10: If the answer to No. 5 is *YES*, then did the defamatory statement injure the Plaintiff?

YES _____
NO _____

Interrogatory No. 11: If the answer to Numbers 1 and 7 is *YES*, then you may assess punitive damages against Defendant. Please indicate the amount of punitive damages, if any, you assess against Defendant:

Amount $ _________

The members of the jury have unanimously answered the Interrogatories in the manner I have indicated.

____
Foreperson

IN THE FIRST JUDICIAL CIRCUIT
IN AND FOR CALUSA COUNTY, XXXXX
CIRCUIT CIVIL DIVISION

CHARISSA WASHINGTON, Individually and as Personal Representative of the Estate of JORDAN AND RONALD WASHINGTON, Deceased, f/b/o any Survivors,

Plaintiff,

v. **Case No. 20XX-1439**

REBECCA HARTWELL,

Defendant.

______________________________________/

SUMMONS

THE STATE OF XXXXX:
TO EACH SHERIFF OF THE STATE:

YOU ARE COMMANDED to serve this summons and a copy of the complaint or petition in this action on defendant:

Rebecca Hartwell
1929 15th Avenue North
Pelican Bay, XXXXX 33707

Each defendant is required to serve written defenses to the complaint or petition on:

Scott Frost, Esq.
Frost, Dunkelheit & Associates, P.L.
412 Central Avenue
Pelican Bay, XXXXX 33707
Plaintiff's Attorney

within 20 days after service of this summons on that defendant, exclusive of the day of service, and to file the original of the defenses with the clerk of this court either before service on plaintiff's attorney or immediately thereafter. If Defendant fails to do so, a default will be entered against that Defendant for the relief demanded in the complaint or petition.

DATED on this 14th day of August 20XX.

Connie Evans
As Clerk of the Court
By Beth Mills
As Deputy Clerk

SUMMONS

IMPORTANT

A lawsuit has been filed against you. You have 20 calendar days after this summons is served on you to file a written response to the attached complaint with the clerk of this court. A phone call will not protect you. Your written response, including the case number given above and the names of the parties, must be filed if you want the court to hear your side of the case. If you do not file your response on time, you may lose the case, and your wages, money, and property may thereafter be taken without further warning from the court. There are other legal requirements. You may want to call an attorney right away. If you do not know an attorney, you may call an attorney referral service or a legal aid office (listed in the phone book).

If you choose to file a written response yourself, at the same time you file your written response to the court you must also mail or take a copy of your written response to the APlaintiff=s Attorney@ named below.

IMPORTANTE

Usted ha sido demando legalmente. Tiene 20 dias, contados a partir del recibo de esta notificacion, para contestar la demanda adjunta, por escrito, y presentarla ante este tribunal. Una llamada telefonica ca no lo protegera. Si usted desea que el tribunal considere su defensa, debe presentar su respuesta por escrito, incluyendo el numero del caso y los nombres de las partes interesadas. Si usted no contesta la demanda a tiempo, puiese perder el caso y podria ser despojado de sus ingresos y propiedades, o privado de sus derechos, sin previo aviso del tribunal. Existen otros requisitos legales. Si lo desea, puede usted consultar a un abogado inmediatamente. Si no conoce a un abogado, puede llamar a una de las oficinas de asistencia legal que aparecen en la guia telefonica.

Si desea responder a la demanda por su cuenta, al mismo tiempo en que presenta su respuesta ante el tribunal, debera usted enviar por correo o entregar una copia de su respuesta a la persona denominada abajo como APlaintiff=s Attorney@ (Demandante o Abogado del Demandante).

IMPORTANTE

De poursuites judiciares ont ete entreprises contre vous. Vous avez 20 jours consecutifs a partir de la date de l=assignation de cette citation pour deposer une reponse ecrite a la plainte ci-jointe aupres de ce tribunal. Un simple coup de telephone est insuffisant pour vous preteger. Vous etes obliges de deposer votre reponse ecrite, avec mention du numero de dossier ci-dessus et du nom des parties nommees ici, si vous souhaitez que le tribunal entende votre cause. Si vous ne desposez pas votre reponse ecrite dans le relai requis, vous risquez de predre la cause ainsi que votre salaire, votre argent, et vos biens peuvent etre saisis par la suite, sans aucun preavis ulterieur du tribunal. Il y a d=autres obligations juridiques et vous pouvez requerir les services immediats d=un avocat. Si vous ne connaissez pas d=avocat, vous pourriez telephoner a un service de reference d=avocats ou a un bureau d=assistance juridique (figurant a l=annuaire de telephones).

Si vous choisissez de deposer vous-meme une reponse ecrite, il vous faudra egalement, en mem temps que cette formalite, faire parvenir ou expedier une copie de votre reponse ecrite au APlaintiff=s Attorney@ (Plaignant ou a son avocat) nomme cidessous.

IN THE FIRST JUDICIAL CIRCUIT
IN AND FOR CALUSA COUNTY, XXXXX
CIRCUIT CIVIL DIVISION

CHARISSA WASHINGTON, Individually and as Personal Representative of the Estate of JORDAN AND RONALD WASHINGTON, Deceased, f/b/o any Survivors,

Plaintiff,

v. **Case No. 20XX-1439**

REBECCA HARTWELL,

Defendant.

______________________________/

COMPLAINT AND DEMAND FOR JURY TRIAL

COMES NOW the Plaintiff, CHARISSA WASHINGTON, Individually, and as Parent and Personal Representative of the Estates of JORDAN WASHINGTON, a minor, and RONALD WASHINGTON, a minor, by and through the undersigned counsel, as and for their Complaint for damages against Defendant, REBECCA HARTWELL, states as follows:

JURISDICTION, PARTIES, AND VENUE

1. This is an action for damages in excess of fifteen thousand dollars ($15,000.00).

2. All conditions precedent to the bringing of this action have occurred or have been performed.

3. At all times material hereto, Plaintiff, CHARISSA WASHINGTON, was and is a resident of Calusa County, XXXXX. Plaintiff, CHARISSA WASHINGTON, was the mother of JORDAN WASHINGTON, deceased and RONALD WASHINGTON, deceased.

4. At all times material hereto, CHARISSA WASHINGTON, was duly appointed as Personal Representative of the Estates of JORDAN WASHINGTON and RONALD WASHINGTON,

5. At all times material hereto, the decedent, JORDAN WASHINGTON, a minor, upon his death left CHARISSA WASHINGTON, his mother, as survivor as defined by XXXXX Stat. § 718.18.

6. At all times material hereto, the decedent, RONALD WASHINGTON, a minor, upon his death left CHARISSA WASHINGTON, his mother, as survivor as defined by XXXXX Stat. § 718.18.

7. At all times material hereto, the Defendant, REBECCA HARTWELL, was and is a resident of Calusa County, XXXXX.

8. On or around March 21, 2008, the Defendant, REBECCA HARTWELL, was operating a Toyota Echo, VIN A610W909O4656B, on 39th Street at or near the University Community Center in Calusa County, XXXXX.

9. At said time, JORDAN WASHINGTON and RONALD WASHINGTON were walking on 39th Street at or near the University Community Center in Pelican Bay, Calusa County, XXXXX.

10. At said time, the Defendant, REBECCA HARTWELL, negligently operated her vehicle, colliding with JORDAN WASHINGTON and RONALD WASHINGTON. JORDAN WASHINGTON and RONALD WASHINGTON were killed as a result of the Defendant's car striking them. Defendant, REBECCA HARTWELL, fled the scene.

11. In no way were JORDAN WASHINGTON and RONALD WASHINGTON responsible for their injuries.

12. Since the death of JORDAN WASHINGTON and RONALD WASHINGTON the Defendant, REBECCA HARTWELL, has continued to make disparaging, public remarks concerning the Plaintiffs.

13. Venue is proper in this action as the subject accident took place in Calusa County, XXXXX.

COUNT I

THE ESTATE'S WRONGFUL DEATH CLAIM OF JORDAN WASHINGTON

14. Plaintiff realleges and reavers paragraphs #1–13 as fully set forth herein and would further state:

15. At all times material hereto, the Defendant, REBECCA HARTWELL, was the owner of the vehicle that struck victim, JORDAN WASHINGTON. As a driver on public roads the Defendant, REBECCA HARTWELL, had a duty to operate her vehicle as a reasonably prudent driver. Defendant, REBECCA HARTWELL, had a duty to exercise reasonable care and to safeguard the public, and in particular the victim, JORDAN WASHINGTON, and refrain from striking him with her motor vehicle.

16. At all times material hereto, the Defendant, REBECCA HARTWELL, breached the aforesaid duty by failing to drive as a reasonably prudent driver and striking the Plaintiff, JORDAN WASHINGTON.

17. As a direct, proximate, and foreseeable result of the negligence of the Defendant, REBECCA HARTWELL, the Plaintiff, JORDAN WASHINGTON, was fatally injured.

18. As a direct, proximate, and foreseeable result of the negligence of the Defendant, REBECCA HARTWELL, the Plaintiff, CHARISSA WASHINGTON, as Personal Representative of the ESTATE OF JORDAN WASHINGTON, deceased, sustained the following losses as set forth in XXXXX Stat. § 768.21:

A. AS TO THE ESTATE OF JORDAN WASHINGTON, DECEASED:

1) Medical and/or funeral expenses due to the decedent's injury/death that would have become a charge against the Estate or that were paid for on behalf of the decedent; and

B. <u>AS TO THE SURVIVING PARENT, CHARISSA WASHINGTON:</u>

1) Value of future lost support and services from the date of the decedent's death with interest;

2) Value of loss of son's companionship;

3) Mental pain and suffering from the date of the injury/death into the future; and

4) Medical and/or funeral expenses due to the decedent's death.

WHEREFORE, Plaintiff, CHARISSA WASHINGTON, as Personal Representative of the ESTATE OF JORDAN WASHINGTON, demands judgment for damages against the Defendant, REBECCA HARTWELL, according to law, together with post-judgment interest and costs, and demands trial by jury of all issues triable as of right by jury.

COUNT II

WRONGFUL DEATH CLAIM OF RONALD WASHINGTON

19. Plaintiff re-alleges and readopts paragraphs #1–13 as fully set forth herein and would further state:

20. At all times material hereto, the Defendant, REBECCA HARTWELL, was the owner of the vehicle that struck Plaintiff, RONALD WASHINGTON. As a driver on public roads the Defendant, REBECCA HARTWELL, had a duty to operate her vehicle as a reasonably prudent driver. Defendant, REBECCA HARTWELL, had a duty to exercise reasonable care and to safeguard the public, and in particular the Plaintiff, RONALD WASHINGTON, and refrain from striking him with her motor vehicle.

21. At all times material hereto, the Defendant, REBECCA HARTWELL, breached the aforesaid duty by failing to drive as a reasonably prudent driver and striking the Plaintiff, RONALD WASHINGTON.

22. As a direct, proximate, and foreseeable result of the negligence of the Defendant, REBECCA HARTWELL, the Plaintiff, RONALD WASHINGTON, was fatally injured.

23. As a direct, proximate, and foreseeable result of the negligence of the Defendant, REBECCA HARTWELL, the Plaintiff, CHARISSA WASHINGTON, as Personal Representative of the ESTATE OF RONALD WASHINGTON, deceased, sustained the following losses as set forth in XXXXX Stat. § 768.21:

A. <u>AS TO THE ESTATE OF RONALD WASHINGTON, DECEASED:</u>

1) Medical and/or funeral expenses due to the decedent's injury/death that would have become a charge against the Estate or that were paid for on behalf of the decedent; and

B. <u>AS TO THE SURVIVING PARENT, CHARISSA WASHINGTON:</u>

1) Value of future lost support and services from the date of the decedent's death with interest;

2) Value of loss of son's companionship;

3) Mental pain and suffering from the date of the injury/death into the future; and

4) Medical and/or funeral expenses due to the decedent's death.

WHEREFORE, Plaintiff, CHARISSA WASHINGTON, as Personal Representative of the ESTATE OF RONALD WASHINGTON, demands judgment for damages against the Defendant, REBECCA HARTWELL, according to law, together with post-judgment interest and costs, and demands trial by jury of all issues triable as of right by jury.

COUNT III

DEFAMATION OF CHARISSA WASHINGTON BY REBECCA HARTWELL

24. Plaintiff realleges and reavers paragraphs #1–11 as fully set forth herein and would further state:

25. Defendant, REBECCA HARTWELL, knowingly made false and defamatory statements to third parties alleging that the Plaintiff, CHARISSA WASHINGTON, was an inferior mother and could not look over her children.

26. These statements were made without reasonable care as to the truth or falsity of the statements. In failing to verify the accuracy of her statements, the Defendant, REBECCA

HARTWELL, acted negligently and/or intentionally knew her statement was not substantially true.

27. The statement exposed the Plaintiff, CHARISSA WASHINGTON, to hatred, ridicule, contempt, embarrassment, humiliation, disgrace, and/or public ridicule within the greater Calusa County Area and throughout the United States.

28. The Defendant's defamatory statements resulted in actual damages and would cause a reasonable person to believe the Plaintiff, CHARISSA WASHINGTON, was and is an incompetent mother.

29. As a direct and proximate result of the defamatory statements made by the Defendant, REBECCA HARTWELL, the Plaintiff, CHARISSA WASHINGTON, has suffered damages resulting from, but not limited to: being shunned in social circles, being unable to function in the public arena, being laughed at and emotionally destroyed by her peers.

WHEREFORE, the Plaintiff, CHARISSA WASHINGTON, demands judgment for damages against the Defendant, REBECCA HARTWELL, together with costs and demands a trial by jury of all issues triable as of right by jury.

Scott Frost

Scott Frost, Esq.
Frost, Dunkelheit & Associates, P.L.
412 Central Avenue
Pelican Bay, XXXXX 33707
(727) 555-3548
XXXXX Bar No. 4521XX
Counsel for Plaintiff

IN THE FIRST JUDICIAL CIRCUIT
IN AND FOR CALUSA COUNTY, XXXXX
CIRCUIT CIVIL DIVISION

CHARISSA WASHINGTON, Individually and as Personal Representative of the Estate of JORDAN AND RONALD WASHINGTON, Deceased, f/b/o any Survivors,

Plaintiff,

v. **Case No. 20XX-1439**

REBECCA HARTWELL,

Defendant.

______________________________/

ANSWER AND AFFIRMATIVE DEFENSES

COMES NOW, the Defendant, REBECCA HARTWELL, by and through the undersigned attorney, and files this Answer to the Plaintiff's Complaint, and as grounds therefore and would state:

1. Denied. Defendant finds the current action unfounded.

2. This paragraph stated legal conclusions to which no response is necessary. To the extent a response is necessary, same are denied.

3. Admitted upon information and belief.

4. Admitted upon information and belief

5. Admitted upon information and belief.

6. Admitted upon information and belief.

7. Admitted for jurisdictional purposes only.

8. Admitted that Defendant, Hartwell, has a Toyota Echo and was driving it on the aforesaid street.

9. Admitted upon information and belief.

10. Denied. After reasonable investigation Defendant is without sufficient knowledge or information to form a belief as to the truth or falsity of the averments contained in this paragraph, therefore same are denied and strict proof to the contrary is demanded at time of trial.

11. Denied. Plaintiffs and their mother are wholly responsible for the unfortunate accident.

12. Denied. After reasonable investigation Defendant is without sufficient knowledge or information to form a belief as to the truth or falsity of the averments contained in this paragraph, therefore same are denied and strict proof to the contrary is demanded at time of trial.

13. Admitted.

COUNT I

NEGLIGENCE OF REBECCA HARTWELL TO JORDAN WASHINGTON

14. Admit in Part. Defendant was the owner and driver of vehicle. Deny in Part. Defendant did not breach said duty.

15. Denied. After reasonable investigation Defendant is without sufficient knowledge or information to form a belief as to the truth or falsity of the averment contained in this paragraph therefore same are denied and strict proof to the contract is demanded at time of trial.

16. Denied. After reasonable investigation Defendant is without sufficient knowledge or information to form a belief as to the truth or falsity of the averments contained in this paragraph, therefore same are denied and strict proof to the contrary is demanded at time of trial.

17. Denied. After reasonable investigation Defendant is without sufficient knowledge or information to form a belief as to the truth or falsity of the averments contained in this paragraph, therefore same are denied and strict proof to the contrary is demanded at time of trial.

COUNT II

NEGLIGENCE OF REBECCA HARTWELL TO RONALD WASHINGTON

18. Denied. After reasonable investigation Defendant is without sufficient knowledge or information to form a belief as to the truth or falsity of the averments contained in this paragraph, therefore same are denied and strict proof to the contrary is demanded at time of trial.

19. Admitted.

20. Denied. After reasonable investigation Defendant is without sufficient knowledge or information to form a belief as to the truth or falsity of the averments contained in this paragraph, therefore same are denied and strict proof to the contrary is demanded at time of trial.

21. Denied. After reasonable investigation Defendant is without sufficient knowledge or information to form a belief as to the truth or falsity of the averments contained in this paragraph, therefore same are denied and strict proof to the contrary is demanded at time of trial.

22. Denied. After reasonable investigation Defendant is without sufficient knowledge or information to form a belief as to the truth or falsity of the averments contained in this paragraph, therefore same are denied and strict proof to the contrary is demanded at time of trial.

23. Defendant is without knowledge and therefore Denied. After reasonable investigation Defendant is without sufficient knowledge or information to form a belief as to the truth or falsity of the averments contained in this paragraph, therefore same are denied and strict proof to the contrary is demanded at time of trial.

24. Defendant is without knowledge and therefore Denied. After reasonable investigation Defendant is without sufficient knowledge or information to form a belief as to the truth or falsity of the averments contained in this paragraph, therefore same are denied and strict proof to the contrary is demanded at time of trial.

COUNT III

DEFAMATION OF CHARISSA WASHINGTON BY REBECCA HARTWELL

25. After reasonable investigation Defendant is without sufficient knowledge or information to form a belief as to the truth or falsity of the averments contained in this paragraph, therefore same are denied and strict proof to the contrary is demanded at time of trial.

26. After reasonable investigation Defendant is without sufficient knowledge or information to form a belief as to the truth or falsity of the averments contained in this paragraph, therefore same are denied and strict proof to the contrary is demanded at time of trial.

27. After reasonable investigation Defendant is without sufficient knowledge or information to form a belief as to the truth or falsity of the averments contained in this paragraph, therefore same are denied and strict proof to the contrary is demanded at time of trial.

28. After reasonable investigation Defendant is without sufficient knowledge or information to form a belief as to the truth or falsity of the averments contained in this paragraph, therefore same are denied and strict proof to the contrary is demanded at time of trial.

29. After reasonable investigation Defendant is without sufficient knowledge or information to form a belief as to the truth or falsity of the averments contained in this paragraph, therefore same are denied and strict proof to the contrary is demanded at time of trial.

30. 28. After reasonable investigation Defendant is without sufficient knowledge or information to form a belief as to the truth or falsity of the averments contained in this paragraph, therefore same are denied and strict proof to the contrary is demanded at time of trial.

FIRST AFFIRMATIVE DEFENSE

The actions of the two deceased children were superseding, intervening causes in whole or in part, to the accident which occurred and damages sustained that absolve the Defendant of liability. In the alternative, Plaintiff was without time to react to the children playing in the street with no lights on. Therefore, Defendant did not breach any duty and is not liable for this accident.

SECOND AFFIRMATIVE DEFENSE

Plaintiff Complaint should be dismissed pursuant to Fed. R. Civ. P. 12(b)(6) for failure to state a claim upon which relief can be granted.

THIRD AFFIRMATIVE DEFENSE

This Defendant is entitled to an apportionment of damages in accordance with Section 768.81 of the XXXXX Statutes. Any judgment entered against this Defendant must be based on the fault, if any, of this Defendant, and not on the basis of the doctrine of joint and several liability. Additionally, the Plaintiffs' recovery must be reduced based upon the percentage of fault attributed to any co-Defendant or any non-party who is found to be at fault for the incident alleged by the Plaintiffs, including but not limited to the Calusa County and Progress Energy. Future discovery will determine what additional parties, if any, were at fault and will be named in accordance with the Fabre and Nash decisions.

FOURTH AFFIRMATIVE DEFENSE

The Plaintiffs have failed to join indispensable parties to this litigation.

FIFTH AFFIRMATIVE DEFENSE

The negligence of the Plaintiff, CHARISSA WASHINGTON, proximately contributed to causing the accident complained of and any resultant damages sustained by Plaintiff, CHARISSA WASHINGTON, because she failed to conduct herself in a reasonable manner and ordinary due care as a parent in supervising her . Thus Plaintiff is barred from recovery herein to the extent that such negligence proximately contributed to causing the complained of accident and/ or any resultant damages sustained by the Plaintiff.

Plaintiff's defamation count is barred by the truth defense.

WHEREFORE, REBECCA HARTWELL, having answered the allegations asserted in the Plaintiff's Complaint, Defendants demand strict proof of all allegations not expressly admitted herein. Further Defendant, REBECCA HARTWELL, demands dismissal of the claims against her and judgment in her favor together with all costs of defense, including attorney's fees, as may be recoverable by law.

Steve Levine, Esquire

Steve Levine & Associates LLP
415 Central Avenue
Pelican Bay, XXXXX 33707
XXXXX Bar No. 453XX
(727)555-7317
Attorney for Defendant

IN THE FIRST JUDICIAL CIRCUIT
IN AND FOR CALUSA COUNTY, XXXXX
CIRCUIT CIVIL DIVISION

CHARISSA WASHINGTON, Individually and as Personal Representative of the Estate of JORDAN AND RONALD WASHINGTON, Deceased, f/b/o any Survivors,

Plaintiff,

v. **Case No. 20XX-1439**

REBECCA HARTWELL,

Defendant.
______________________________________/

PLAINTIFF=S FIRST REQUEST FOR PRODUCTION OF DOCUMENTS TO DEFENDANT, REBECCA HARTWELL

Pursuant to XXXXX Rule of Civil Procedure 1.350(a), Plaintiff, CHARISSA WASHINGTON., requests that Defendant, REBECCA HARTWELL, respond to the following requests for documents within forty-five (45) days after service of process. Plaintiff further requests that said documents be produced for inspection and photocopying at the office of Frost, Dunkelheit & Associates, P.L., 412 Central Avenue, Pelican Bay, XXXXX 33707 forty-five days from the date of service of this request. If the date and time of inspection are inconvenient, please promptly contact the undersigned attorney to reschedule. Alternatively, photocopies of the requested documents may be mailed by said date to the aforesaid address in lieu of the inspection.

DEFINITIONS

1. As used herein, the terms "you" and "your" shall mean Defendant, REBECCA HARTWELL.

2. As used herein, the phrase "accident" shall mean the collision of defendant's 20XX-5 Toyota Echo and the Five Children of Ms. Charissa Washington that occurred on March 21, 20XX-2, as alleged in the Complaint and Demand for Jury Trial.

3. As used herein, the term "document(s)" is defined as follows. One, the term refers to all writings of any kind, including originals and all non-identical copies, whether different from the original by reason of any notation made on such copies or otherwise. Two, the term "document(s)" includes the following without limitation: correspondence, memoranda, notes, diaries, statistics, letters, materials, invoices, orders, directives, interviews, telegrams, minutes, reports, studies, statements, transcripts, summaries, pamphlets, books, intraoffice and interoffice communications, notations of conversation, telephone call records, bulletins, printed forms,

teletype, telefax, worksheets, electronic mail, e-mail, and regularly-kept records. Three, the term "document(s)" also includes the following without limitation: photographs, digital images, charts, graphs, microfiche, microfilm, videotape, audiotape, motion pictures, computer data, and information contained on a fixed or floppy computer disc.

REQUESTS

Please produce the following:

1. All photographs and/or digital images of decedents taken after the auto accident.

2. All photographs and/or digital images of your vehicle taken after the auto accident.

3. All photographs and/or digital images of the accident scene taken after the auto accident.

4. All repair estimates for damage to your vehicle arising from the auto accident.

5. All documents showing who owned the vehicle which you drove in the auto accident.

6. All documents showing whether you were acting within the course and scope of your employment at the time of the auto accident.

7. All documents which you contend would support your affirmative defenses.

8. All of your insurance coverage documents for all auto policies, umbrella policies, or excess policies which may provide coverage for the auto accident.

9. All recorded statements taken by you related to the auto accident.

10. All witness statements received by you related to the auto accident.

11. Paperwork establishing ownership of defendant's dance studio.

12. Copies of all newspaper clippings kept by defendant, defendant's family, or by others at the request of the defendant concerning the accident and death of Jordan and Ronald Washington.

<u>Scott Frost, Esquire</u>

Scott Frost, Esq.
Frost, Dunkelheit & Associates, P.L.
412 Central Avenue
Pelican Bay, XXXXX 33707
(727) 555-3548
XXXXX Bar No. 4521XX
Counsel for Plaintiff

IN IN THE FIRST JUDICIAL CIRCUIT
IN AND FOR CALUSA COUNTY, XXXXX
CIRCUIT CIVIL DIVISION

CHARISSA WASHINGTON, Individually and as Personal Representative of the Estate of JORDAN AND RONALD WASHINGTON, Deceased, f/b/o any Survivors,

Plaintiff,

v. **Case No. 20XX-1439**

REBECCA HARTWELL,

Defendant.
______________________________________/

PLAINTIFF'S FIRST SET OF INTERROGATORIES

Pursuant to XXXXX Rule of Civil Procedure 1.340(a), Plaintiff, CHARISSA WASHINGTON, hereby requests that Defendant, REBECCA HARTWELL, answer the following Interrogatory Numbers 1-10 under oath within forty-five (45) days after service of process.

DEFINITIONS

1. As used herein, the terms "you" and "your" shall mean Defendant, REBECCA HARTWELL.

2. As used herein, the phrase "auto accident" shall mean the striking of children on 39th street on March 21, 20XX-2 as alleged in the Complaint and Demand for Jury Trial.

Scott Frost

Scott Frost, Esq.
Frost, Dunkelheit & Associates, P.L.
412 Central Avenue
Pelican Bay, XXXXX 33707
(727) 555-3548
XXXXX Bar No. 4521XX
Counsel for Plaintiff

INTERROGATORIES TO DEFENDANT, REBECCA HARTWELL

1. Please state the full legal name(s) and physical address(es) of each and every person who owned the vehicle which you were operating at the time of the auto accident.

   Rebecca Hartwell
   1929 15th Avenue North
   Pelican Bay, XXXXXX 33707

2. Were you acting within the course and scope of your employment at the time of the auto accident? If and only if your answer is yes, please state the complete legal name of your employer, your employer's physical business address, your job title, and your dates of employment for that employer.

   No

3. Describe any and all policies of insurance which you contend cover or may cover you for the allegations set forth in Plaintiff's Complaint, detailing as to such policies the name of the insurer, the policy number, the effective dates of the policy, the available limits of liability, and the name and address of the custodian of the policy.

   GEICO – liability limit is 300,000 dollars.
   Policy Number - 5673901-12
   Effective Dates – December 2, 20xx-3 through June 2, 20xx-2
   GEICO of XXXXXX
   1820 Bayshore Hills
   Pelican Bay, XXXXXX 33453

4. Were you married at the time of the auto accident? If and only if your answer is yes, please state the full legal name of your husband, his last known residential address, the date of your marriage to him, and the state of your marriage.

No – never married.

5. State the facts upon which you rely for each affirmative defense in your Answer.

Upon the advice of counsel I direct you to review their written response as my agent to this interrogatory.

6. Do you contend any person or entity other than you is, or may be, liable in whole or part for the claims asserted against you in this lawsuit? If so, state the full name and address of each such person or entity, the legal basis for your contention, the facts or evidence upon which your contention is based, and whether or not you have notified each such person or entity of your contention.

Upon the advice of counsel I direct you to review their written response as my agent to this interrogatory.

7. Do you contend that any individual or entity not named as a party to this action was at fault, in whole or in part, in causing or contributing to cause the subject incident or subject injuries? If so, state the full name and address of each such person or entity, the legal basis for your contention, the facts or evidence upon which your contention is based, and whether or not you have notified each such person or entity of your contention.

Upon the advice of counsel I direct you to review their written response as my agent to this interrogatory.

8. List the names and addresses of all persons who are believed or known by you, your agents or attorneys to have any knowledge concerning any of the issues in this lawsuit; and specify the subject matter about which the witness has knowledge.

Upon the advice of counsel I direct you to review their written response as my agent to this interrogatory.

9. Describe in detail each act or omission on the part of any party to this lawsuit that you contend constituted negligence that was a contributing legal cause of the incident in question.

Upon the advice of counsel I direct you to review their written response as my agent to this interrogatory.

10. To the best of your recollection, please set forth the following:

a. the date of the auto accident. *March 21, 20XX-2.*
b. the time of the auto accident. *7:15 p.m.*
c. the weather conditions at the time of the auto accident. *Sun had just gone down, it was hot, dry.*
d. what you saw happen to the five children immediately after the collision. *I never saw the children until they struck my windshield and car door.*

OATH OF DEFENDANT, REBECCA HARTWELL

STATE OF *XXXXX*

COUNTY OF *Calusa*

I, REBECCA HARTWELL, am the Defendant in this lawsuit and hereby swear by my notarized signature below that the Answers to Plaintiff's Interrogatory Numbers 1-10 are both true and correct to the best of my personal knowledge.

DEFENDANT:

Rebecca Hartwell

SIGNATURE OF REBECCA HARTWELL

REBECCA HARTWELL, who is either personally known to the undersigned Notary Public or has produced XXXXX Driver's License Number as identification, appeared and signed these Interrogatory Answers under oath on the 5th day of May 20XX.

Vilma Rodriguez

Vilma Rodriguez
NOTARY PUBLIC
STATE OF XXXXX
My Commission Expires: October XX, 20XX +2

Offense Incident Report # 20XX(-2)10101

Pelican Bay Police Department

Investigator: James Record

Subject: Accident Scene on 39st Street Near the University Center, called in by a 9-1-1 call.

Address: 39th Street – between 15th and 15th Avenue South, Pelican Bay

Felony: Vehicular Homicide

Victim(s): Ronald Washington, Jordan Washington, Laquinta Washington, August Washington, Charles Washington

Narrative

Page 1 of 3.

Responded to a radio dispatch- investigate a hit and run involving three children on 15st Avenue South and 39st Street. Area is dangerous part of town – drug dealers, bad living areas, homeless folks, very violent area of town. Upon arrival I saw what appeared to be two different large gangs of people milling around, screaming, throwing beer bottles and shouting for revenge. There was one other person already there in uniform but I did not get their badge number or precinct. I arrived within three minutes of the call, but crowds had already gathered. It was an ugly crowd scene. Spent at least 45 minutes getting people out of the accident area. They kept coming back, walking around, moving pieces of the debris. I had to arrest one person for picking up what they described as "evidence" of the crime. There were plastic, glass, and metal car parts scattered in the road. I saw both sneakers and sandals that had been knocked loose from feet. They appeared to be in the southbound lane.

The first victim I approached was an adolescent boy lying on the pavement near the center stripe. He wasn't moving and his head and mouth were bleeding. The second victim, a little girl, was a few feet away from the boy, to the west. She was laying in the southbound lane. She was badly hurt with a broken leg, but was talking. She kept saying "the big white van hit me." I could not be sure how many bodies there were. Farther up the street, people were yelling, "there's two more up here!" The people had moved the third victim; it was little boy no more than 3 years old. He wasn't moving. He was on the center line of 39st Street.

PELICAN BAY POLICE DEPARTMENT
CALUSA COUNTY, FLORIDA

ARREST NUMBER: n/a

COMPLAINT NUMBER: 20XX(-2)10101

NARRATIVE (cont'd):

Page 2 of 3.

It looked like the boy was dragged about 150 feet by the vehicle going northbound. There was a fourth child but we couldn't tell how badly hurt he was because the street lights were not working. Three ambulances and a rescue chopper rushed the children to a local hospital.

We only secured the scene after the rescue efforts were completed. The crowds were angry and it took a great deal of time to control them. We marked plastic car parts, metal car parts, sneakers, and sandals. We didn't really know what we were looking for or what would be important, there was so much debris. I found Toyota parts and parts from a Honda Accord. Some of them were on the road and some were laying on the side of the road by the Royal Garden Apartments.

There was debris everywhere. I watched as several groups of folks moved pieces of the accident debris around. I stopped them but was not able to get everything back into its original location.

I took witness statements from Johnny Broadsides, Dimitri Merinov and Matt Bader. Another boy whose name I did not get said that he remembered sitting on the bench when he saw a white van speeding, then he heard a loud boom. A 13-year-old remembered the children standing on the grass between the sidewalk and the road. They were holding hands, as if they were about to cross the street.

PELICAN BAY POLICE DEPARTMENT
CALUSA COUNTY, FLORIDA

ARREST NUMBER: n/a

COMPLAINT NUMBER: 20XX(-2)10101

NARRATIVE (cont'd):

Page 3 of 3.

A few seconds later the teen saw the children tumbling over a white van like dominoes. He did not see any other vehicle strike the children.

Several witnesses said two vehicles were involved and a few said that three were involved. Stories varied. One said that a Honda dragged a child down the street before flipping off its lights and speeding away. People did not agree on the models or their makes, which direction they were traveling, which ones had actually struck the children. No one got a license plate number. I received different descriptions and it appears at this time that at least two, if not three, vehicles were involved.

One witness saw a dark Toyota strike the youngest child, drag him around 150 feet, stop, turn off their lights, turn on their lights and then leave.

Investigation will continue by accident reconstruction technicians.

Attached files: 1. Sketch of the Accident Scene,Photos, statements of Broadsides and Merinov

REPORTING OFFICER	James Record	DATE REPORTED	22 Mar 20XX-2
REPORTING OFFICER	James Record (SIGNATURE)	BR549 (OFFICER BADGE)	22 Mar 20XX-2 (DATE)
REVIEWING SUPERVISOR	Robert Burrell (SIGNATURE)	BR9240 (OFFICER BADGE)	22 Mar 20XX-2 (DATE)

CALUSA POLICE DEPARTMENT
CALUSA COUNTY

INVESTIGATION REPORT

Report No	Date:	Complaining Witness:
20XX-203230355	3/23/20XX-02	Charissa Washington

Investigating Officer:	Suspect:
Detective Edwin Morris	Rebecca Hartwell
Division:	**Address:**
Homicide	Royal Garden Apartments

Victim(s):	Age(s):	General Description:
Ronald Washington, Jordan Washington	14, 3	Two African American males, ages 14 and 3

Investigator's Notes:

March 23, 20XX-2:

Case assigned to Homicide division. Opened case file, began investigation.

On March 21, 20XX:-2 Officer James Record responded to an accident scene. They were called in to deal with a hit and run that resulted in the death of two children. Chief Hightower assigned case to my division on March 23, 20XX-2. No accident scene reconstruction was conducted the day of the accident, and the video of the scene was destroyed by Officer Record when he inadvertently incorrectly attempted to download the materials to his department laptop. Investigation plan includes developing diagrams, interviewing witnesses and securing evidence if available. Inserted transcript of 911 call (exhibit 1) and photos of oldest child into case file (exhibits 2, 3, and 4).
Investigation continues.

March 28, 20XX-2.
Developed diagrams of the relevant areas (exhibit 5, 6 and 7 of this report)
Secured overhead shots of accident area from Google Maps(exhibits 8 and 9)
Secured street shot of accident area by basketball court from Google Maps (exhibit 10)
Inserted Sun Up and Sun Down Report into the case file (exhibit 11)
Interviewed Bill Hartwell.
Interviewed Marian Hartwell.
Investigation continues.

April 7, 20XX-2.
Received statements from Johnny Broadsides (exhibit 12) and Dimitri Merinov (exhibit 13) from Officer Record. Reviewed and inserted into the case file.

May 12, 20XX-2.
Statements given by Mr. Hartwell (exhibit 14) and Mrs. Hartwell (exhibit 15) on 28 March returned by their attorney Steve Levine. Placed in the file once received.

CALUSA POLICE DEPARTMENT
CALUSA COUNTY

INVESTIGATION REPORT

July 7, 20XX-2.
Located Mr. Bader, brought him in for questioning. He provided a statement (exhibit 16). He also provided two video files from his cell phone that night (exhibits 17 and 18). Procured MP3 of the 911 call (exhibit 19) Requested an additional statement from Officer Record.

July 13, 20XX-2. Officer Record provides affidavit (exhibit 20).

Subsequent investigation revealed that probable cause exists to believe that Rebecca Hartwell drove the vehicle that struck both Ronald and Jordan Washington on the night of 21 March 20XX-2.
Investigation continues.

July 13, 20XX-1. Hung jury in the case of State v. Hartwell. Case file closed.

/--Nothing Follows--/

Sworn and subscribed in my presence, July 13, 20XX-1. Signature: Edwin Morris	I swear and affirm that the report above and the attached files are true and correct to the best of my Belief and Knowledge.
Supervisor: Robert Burrell Supervisor's Signature Robert Burrell	Signature: Edwin Morris
Case Status: Closed — Date:072320XX-1	

Transcript of 911 Call
21 March 20XX-2
7:17 p.m.

1. **OPERATOR**: This is 911, what is your emergency?

2. **CALLER**: I'm at the University Community Center on 39th Street and I just saw an accident. You guys need to get out here right now, man.

3. **OPERATOR**: Sir, please describe what happened.

4. **CALLER**: I was playing basketball down here and just a second ago I just heard an accident. There's…aww man…there's like three kids just got hit by a car. And, and, I think there might be another that got hit too. Hurry up and get down here! I think these kids are dying!

5. **OPERATOR**: Sir, how many vehicles were involved?

6. **CALLER**: I don't know, there was one stopped here like it was involved in it or something and another stopped further down the road. It started its engine and sped off. I think that one was involved.

7. **OPERATOR**: So, both vehicles have left?

8. **CALLER**: Yeah! They both just took off!

9. **OPERATOR**: Can you please describe those vehicles sir?

10. **CALLER**: I dunno. I'm pretty sure the one stopped here closer to the Center was a Ford Econoline Van, white I think. The other one looked like a small Toyota or Honda, some dark color or something.

11. **OPERATOR**: Sir, the police and paramedics should be arriving very soon, they may need your assistance when they arrive so please remain calm and stay where you are, OK?

12. **CALLER**: OK Just hurry up!

I hereby certify that the above transcript is a true and accurate copy of the tape maintained on file in the office of the emergency response center, Calusa County Sherriff's Department, Pelican Bay, Florida.

Charlotte Jones
Administrative Clerk
Calusa County Sherriff's Department
May 6, 20XX-2

Exhibit 1

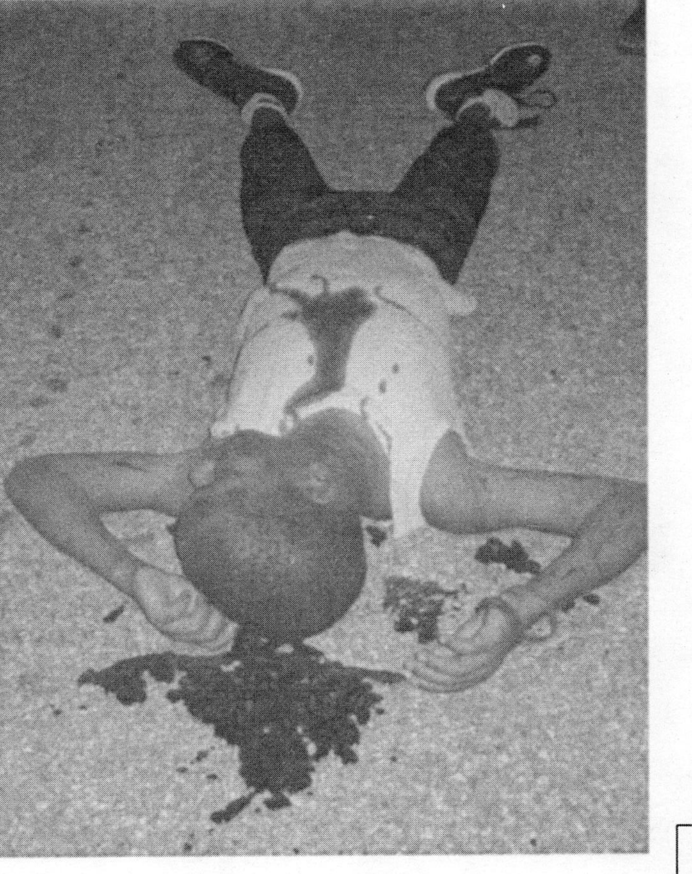

Exhibit 2

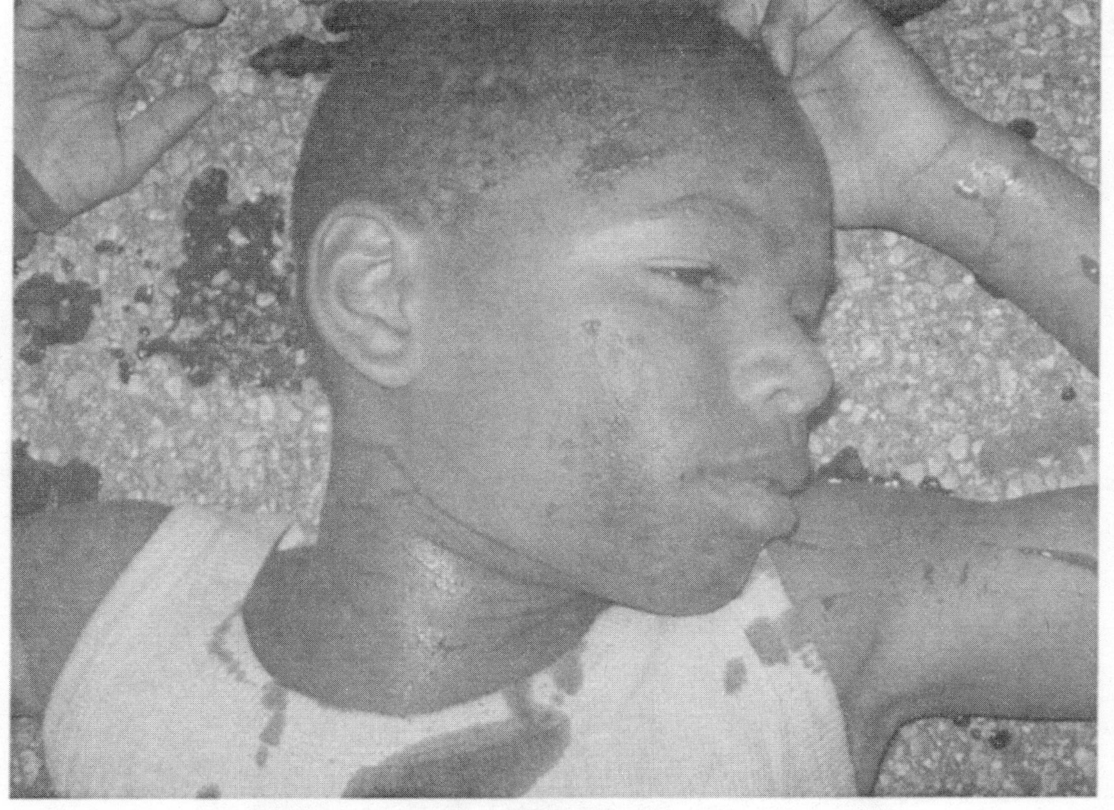

Exhibit 3

Exhibit 4

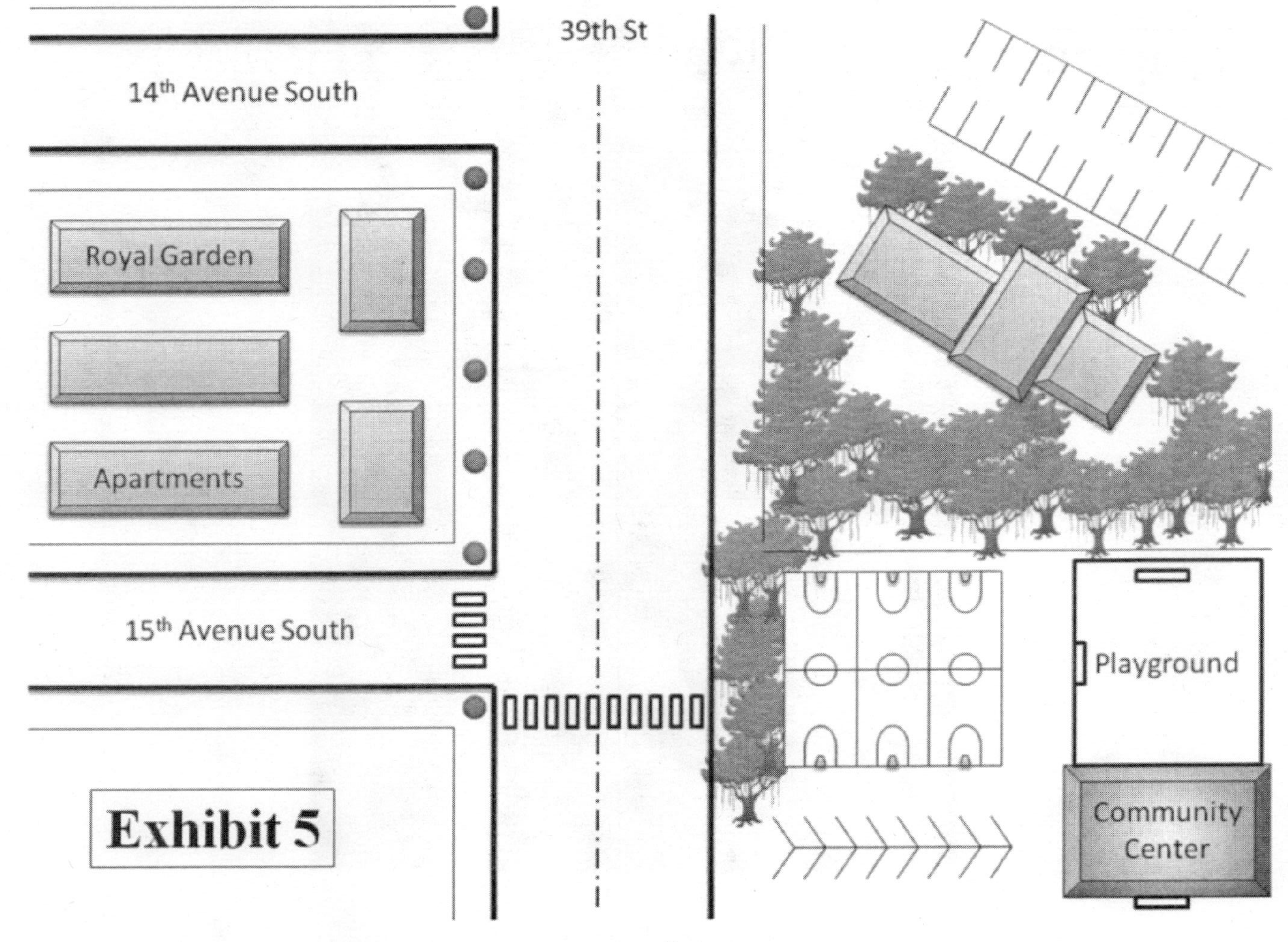
39th St
14th Avenue South
Royal Garden
Apartments
15th Avenue South
Exhibit 5
Playground
Community
Center

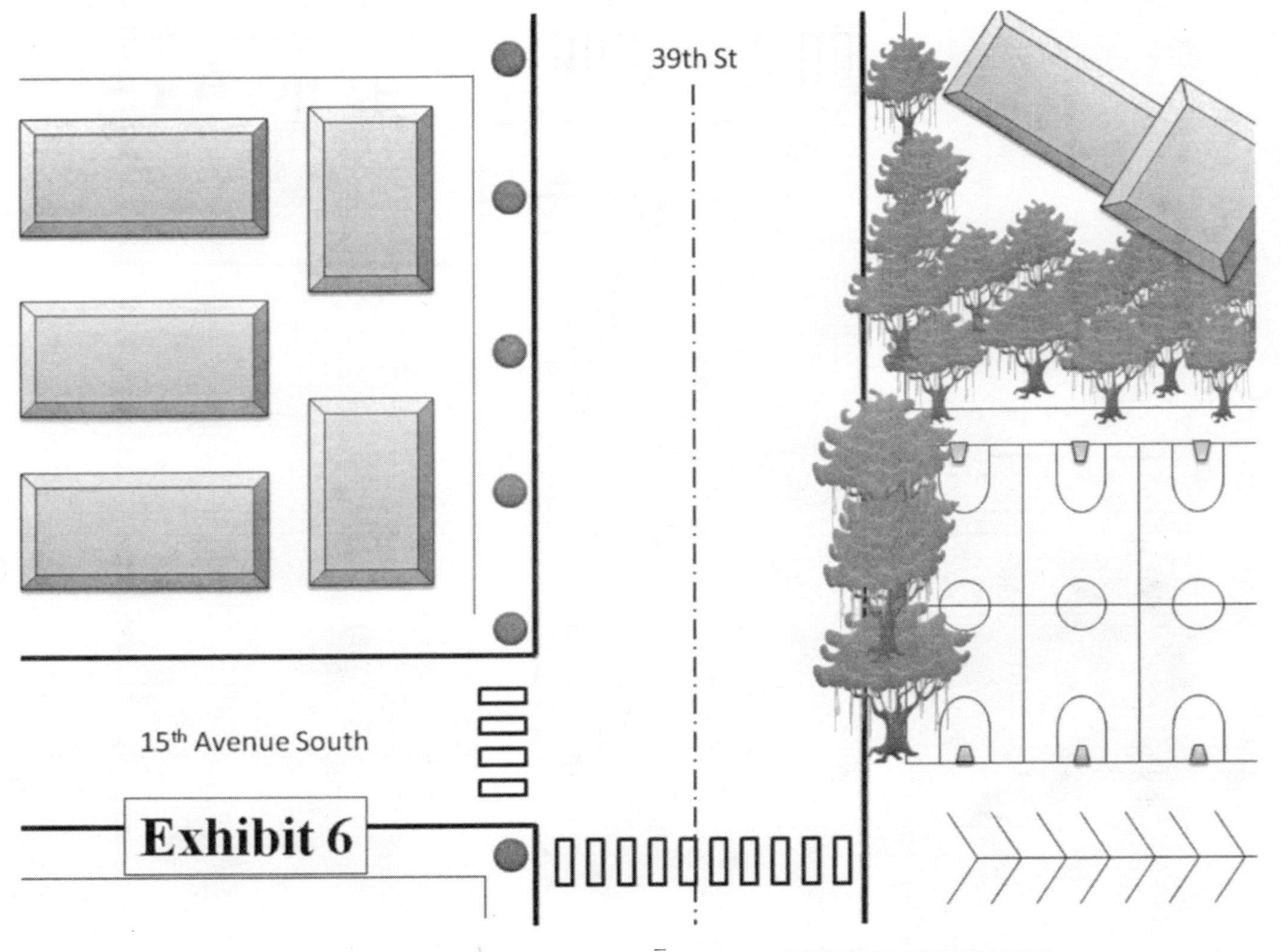
39th St
15th Avenue South
Exhibit 6

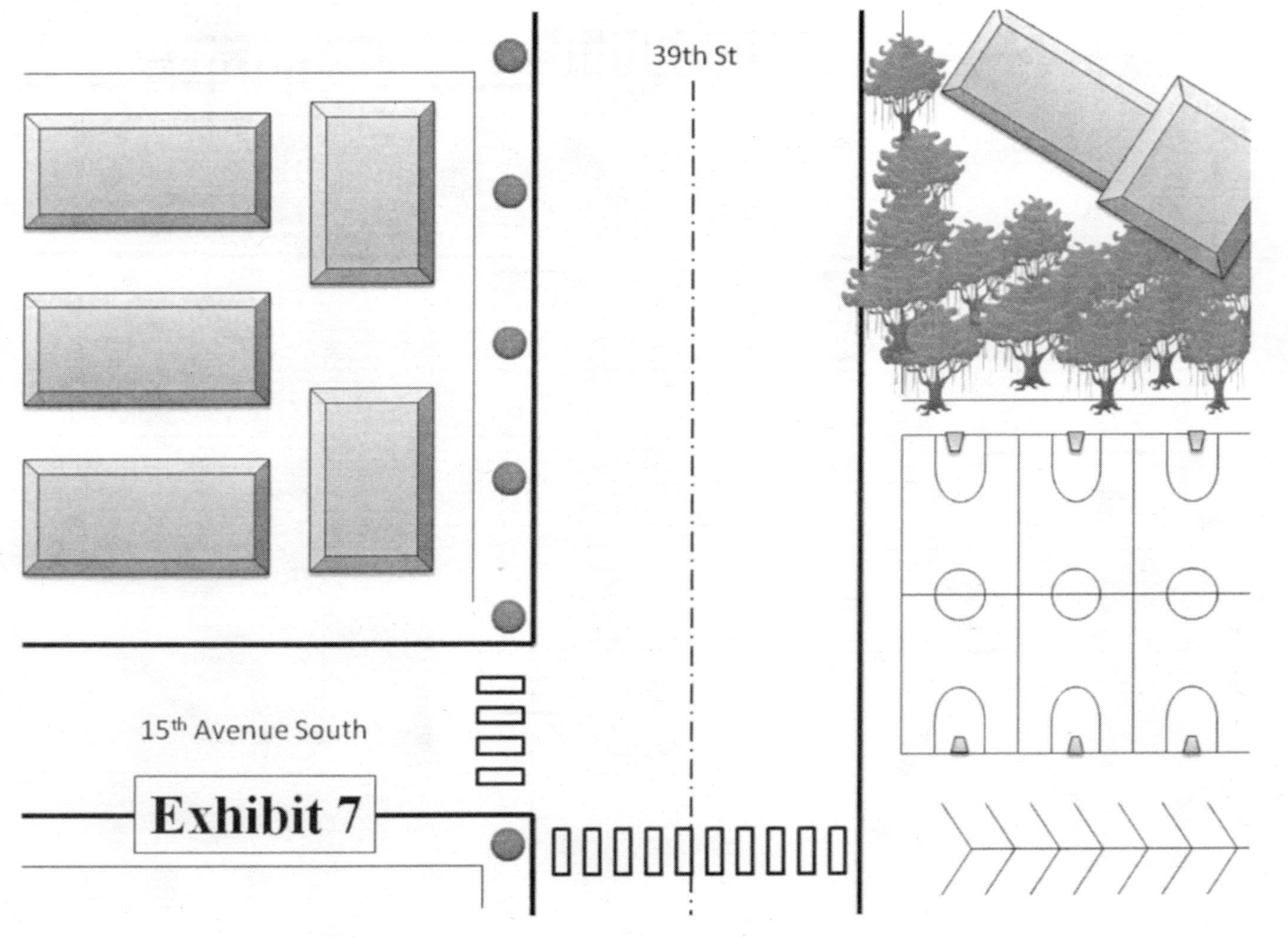
39th St
15th Avenue South
Exhibit 7

Exhibit 8

Exhibit9

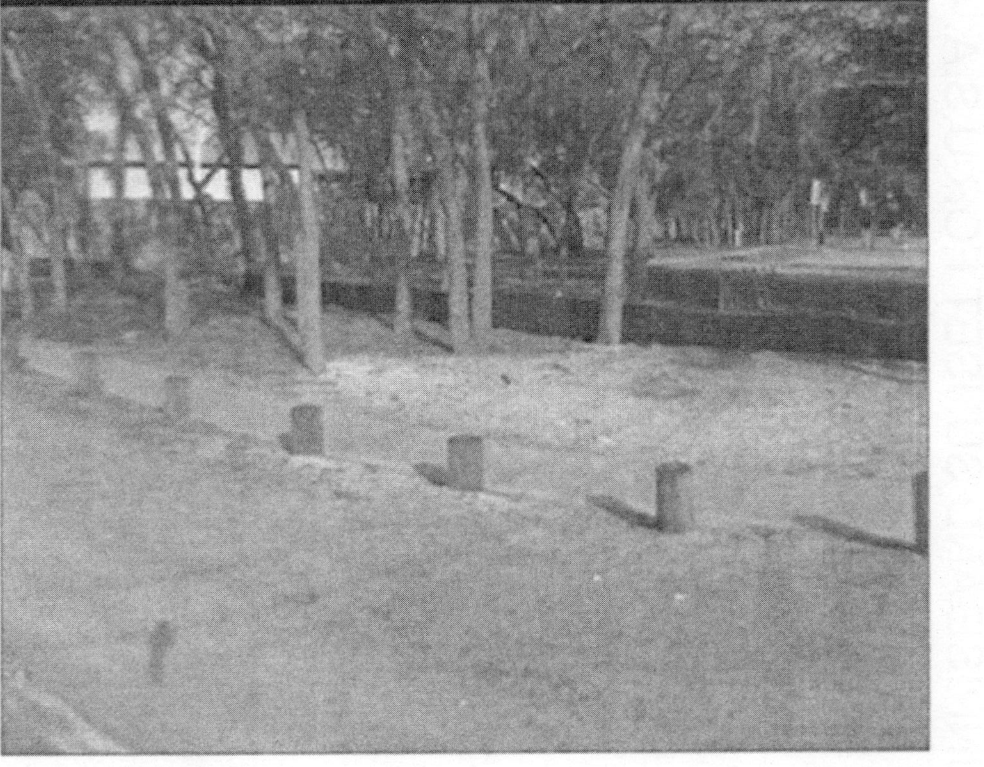

Exhibit 10

Register | Log in | Customize

Search: [ ] Go

Current location: Home page > Time zone menu > The World Clock > Sun Calculator > Results

Other locations: Date menu | Calendar | Countdown

SUNRISE AND SUNSET FOR U.S.A. – PELICAN BAY – MARCH 20XX-2

Time/General
Weather
Time zone
DST
Sun & Moon

Pelican Bay, XXXXX, United States

Rising and setting times for the Sun

Date	Sunrise	Sunset	Length of day		Solar noon		
			This day	Difference	Time	Altitude	Distance (10^6 km)
Mar 1, 20XX-2	6:55 AM	6:31 PM	11h 35m 18s	+ 1m 38s	12:43 PM	54.5°	148.223
Mar 2, 20XX-2	6:54 AM	6:31 PM	11h 36m 56s	+ 1m 38s	12:43 PM	54.9°	148.259
Mar 3, 20XX-2	6:53 AM	6:32 PM	11h 38m 34s	+ 1m 38s	12:42 PM	55.3°	148.296
Mar 4, 20XX-2	6:52 AM	6:33 PM	11h 40m 13s	+ 1m 38s	12:42 PM	55.7°	148.333
Mar 5, 20XX-2	6:51 AM	6:33 PM	11h 41m 52s	+ 1m 38s	12:42 PM	56.0°	148.371
Mar 6, 20XX-2	6:50 AM	6:34 PM	11h 43m 31s	+ 1m 39s	12:42 PM	56.4°	148.410
Mar 7, 20XX-2	6:49 AM	6:34 PM	11h 45m 11s	+ 1m 39s	12:42 PM	56.8°	148.448
Mar 8, 20XX-2	6:48 AM	6:35 PM	11h 46m 50s	+ 1m 39s	12:41 PM	57.2°	148.488
Mar 9, 20XX-2	6:47 AM	6:36 PM	11h 48m 30s	+ 1m 39s	12:41 PM	57.6°	148.528
Mar 10, 20XX-2	6:46 AM	6:36 PM	11h 50m 10s	+ 1m 39s	12:41 PM	58.0°	148.568
Mar 11, 20XX-2	6:45 AM	6:37 PM	11h 51m 50s	+ 1m 40s	1:41 PM	58.4°	148.609
Mar 12, 20XX-2	6:44 AM	6:37 PM	11h 53m 30s	+ 1m 40s	1:40 PM	58.8°	148.649
Mar 13, 20XX-2	6:43 AM	6:38 PM	11h 55m 11s	+ 1m 40s	1:40 PM	59.2°	148.690
Mar 14, 20XX-2	6:42 AM	6:38 PM	11h 56m 51s	+ 1m 40s	1:40 PM	59.6°	148.732
Mar 15, 20XX-2	7:40 AM	7:39 PM	11h 58m 32s	+ 1m 40s	1:39 PM	60.0°	148.773

Mar 16, 20XX-2	6:39 AM	6:40 PM	12h 00m 12s	+ 1m 40s	1:39 PM	60.4°	148.814
Mar 17, 20XX-2	6:38 AM	6:40 PM	12h 01m 53s	+ 1m 40s	1:39 PM	60.7°	148.856
Mar 18, 20XX-2	6:37 AM	6:41 PM	12h 03m 34s	+ 1m 40s	1:39 PM	61.1°	148.897
Mar 19, 20XX-2	6:36 AM	6:41 PM	12h 05m 14s	+ 1m 40s	1:38 PM	61.5°	148.939
Mar 20, 20XX-2	6:35 AM	6:42 PM	12h 06m 55s	+ 1m 40s	1:38 PM	61.9°	148.980
Mar 21, 20XX-2	7:34 AM	6:42 PM	12h 08m 36s	+ 1m 40s	1:38 PM	62.3°	149.021
Mar 22, 20XX-2	7:33 AM	7:43 PM	12h 10m 16s	+ 1m 40s	1:37 PM	62.7°	149.063
Mar 23, 20XX-2	7:31 AM	7:43 PM	12h 11m 57s	+ 1m 40s	1:37 PM	63.1°	149.104
Mar 24, 20XX-2	7:30 AM	7:44 PM	12h 13m 37s	+ 1m 40s	1:37 PM	63.5°	149.146
Mar 25, 20XX-2	7:29 AM	7:44 PM	12h 15m 18s	+ 1m 40s	1:37 PM	63.9°	149.187
Mar 26, 20XX-2	7:28 AM	7:45 PM	12h 16m 58s	+ 1m 40s	1:36 PM	64.3°	149.229
Mar 27, 20XX-2	7:27 AM	7:45 PM	12h 18m 38s	+ 1m 40s	1:36 PM	64.7°	149.270
Mar 28, 20XX-2	7:26 AM	7:46 PM	12h 20m 18s	+ 1m 40s	1:36 PM	65.1°	149.312
Mar 29, 20XX-2	7:25 AM	7:47 PM	12h 21m 58s	+ 1m 39s	1:35 PM	65.5°	149.354
Mar 30, 20XX-2	7:23 AM	7:47 PM	12h 23m 38s	+ 1m 39s	1:35 PM	65.9°	149.396
Mar 31, 20XX-2	7:22 AM	7:48 PM	12h 25m 18s	+ 1m 39s	1:35 PM	66.2°	149.439

All times are in local time for Pelican Bay

Note that Daylight Saving Time started on March 22, 20XX-2 at 2:00 AM and this is accounted for above. March Equinox (Vernal Equinox) is on Tuesday, March 20, 20XX-2 at 7:07 PM in Pelican Bay.

- Time and Date uses the tables of times for sunrise and sunset provided by the National Weather Service.

Exhibit 11

Exhibit 12

Officer Initials: JR

PELICAN BAY POLICE DEPARTMENT
CALUSA COUNTY, FLORIDA

VOLUNTARY STATEMENT
(NOT UNDER ARREST)
PAGE 52 OF 2

My name is Johnny Broadsides. I am 17 years old.

At the time of this statement, I am not under arrest nor am I being investigated for the commission of any crime or offense. I have given this statement voluntarily and I offer this information for whatever purpose it may serve.

On March 21, 20XX-2 I saw and heard some of what happened in the accident outside the University Community Center. I worked the night before, so I didn't get up on the 21st till around 3 in the afternoon. I hung out with my boys on the street corner most of the afternoon and then we went over to the community center courts to play some b-ball. We'd been playing for around two hours when we all heard this horrible thud and kids screaming. We ran up the street looking for what happened. I say a white van stopped in the road pretty close to the b-ball courts and up the road around 100 feet or so were two cars, a Toyota and some kind of Honda. Kids were lying in the street, looking like something you would see on the tv screen from Baghdad. Blood was everywhere. I'm pretty fast so I ran up to the Honda and began beating on the window telling them to get out. The person inside, I think it was a woman, freaked out and took off. She almost ran my foot over! I then ran up about another 10 feet to the Toyota. There was this baby lying in the road and it looked so bad.... I started screaming and hollering at the Toyota. It peeled out of there before I got a chance to see who was driving it, but I remember seeing blood and other stuff smeared all over the left side of that car. It was awful. I have never been in trouble with the law and I don't know none of them kids. Best that way I suppose cause it might be too hard to take if I could put a name to the baby's fact. Still keeps me up at night. Some folks should not be in our neighborhood when they don't belong. It just ain't right – they better watch out cause sometimes things happen to folks who don't belong here. You know how things are down here.

I certify that the facts given in this statement consist of 2 pages and are correct to the best of my knowledge. I have reviewed this statement and signed my name below.

Johnny Broadsides

Signature of person giving statement

Witness

March 23, 20XX-2

Date

Witness

Official Use Only		
Lt. James Record	James Record	
Officer (Printed Name)	Officer Signature	Date

JB

Exhibit 13

Officer Initials: JR

PELICAN BAY POLICE DEPARTMENT
CALUSA COUNTY, FLORIDA

VOLUNTARY STATEMENT
(NOT UNDER ARREST)
PAGE 54 OF 2

My name is Dimitri Merinov. I am 24 years old.

At the time of this statement, I am not under arrest nor am I being investigated for the commission of any crime or offense. I have given this statement voluntarily and I offer this information for whatever purpose it may serve.

On March 21, 20XX-2 I saw and heard some of what happened in the accident outside the University Community Center. I got off of work at the United Express sorting facility at about 12:00p that afternoon. I worked an early shift from 4:00a to 12:00p. I was going to play in a 3-on-3 basketball tournament that night at the Community Center, so when I came home from work I wanted to sleep for a few hours. I woke up and got ready a little before 5:30. My game started at 6:00 and I got there about 10 minutes before that. When I was playing I noticed the four kids who were involved in the accident at the park watching the games. I recognized them because they live next to me in my building. I played my game and finished at 6:50. A little after 7:00 I was cooling off and talking with a few people when I heard like a muffled "boom, boom" come from the street in front of the Community Center. I grabbed

Page 1 of 3 D.M.

my camera phone from my bag and ran out there. I could see that two vehicles were stopped in the road both going the same direction I guess. One was a white panel van and the other was a dark colored Toyota and they were pretty far apart. The van was a little closer to me and when I got there it was driving slowly and then sped off. The Toyota was about 150 feet down the road and it had stopped. I know it was a manual transmission because it looked like it stalled out because it stared again I heard the gears grinding before it finally lurched and sped off. I got video of it with my camera phone. I walked into the street and saw the three of the neighbor kids I recognized hurt badly in the road, but the fourth wasn't with them. It looked like they got hit. I heard bystanders say that they saw the van and the Toyota hit them. Someone screamed from where the Toyota was stopped and said that there was another of the kids down there about 150 feet away. Some other people said that the Toyota dragged the kid all the way down the street to where it stopped. I"m really upset because I know these kids and their mother. Monique Washington is my neighbor and a good friend of mine. I heard her crying and upset all day the next day when she came home. I stopped by her house to check on her and she told me two of her kids died. She said she thought it was "all her fault." I guess I should tell you

 D.M.

that I have a criminal record. About five years ago I was convicted of petit theft here in Pelican Bay. About four years ago I was convicted of trespassing. I'm working hard now at my job and trying I'm trying get past all that.

I certify that the facts given in this statement consist of 3 pages and are correct to the best of my knowledge. I have reviewed this statement and signed my name below.

Dimitri Merinov
Signature of person giving statement

Witness

March 23, 20XX-2
Date

Witness

Official Use Only		
Lt. James Record	James Record	
Officer (Printed Name)	Officer Signature	Date

JB

BH Page 1 of 3

Exhibit 14

My name is Bill Hartwell. I've worked as a postal worker since 1979. I'm married to my wonderful wife, Marian, and we live in Pelican Bay in Calusa County, FL. We have two daughters, Rebecca, 28, and Gina, 23. My wife moved here from Cuba as a little girl. But both of my daughters grew up here in Calusa County. We are a tight-knit family, and my girls are wonderful children. And smart, too. As babies they only spoke Spanish. It wasn't until Rebecca went to pre-school that she learned English. But she was a great student all the way from her time at St. Mary's Elementary School through high school. She always made 'A's and 'B's at Incarnation High.

As kids Rebecca and Gina were constantly dancing. Probably since Rebecca was 8, she was doing ballet. The girls absolutely loved it. They took it serious, and I could tell they were serious about it. I even converted our garage into a dance studio. Wooden slab floor, a wall of mirrors, it even had the ballet bar. I did it all in a single weekend. The kids loved it. I used to watch them practice, and I'd give them pointers. I would tell them if they forgot to point their toes when they jumped. I had a pretty good eye for those sorts of things.

And it must have helped, too. Rebecca is a dance teacher at Northside Elementary Magnet School. She also has her own studio. She is the owner/director of the Dance, Dance, Dance Studio. Her studio is located Pelican Bay, about 5 miles from the University Community Center. Pelican Bay Her students loved her. They really looked up to her and admired her. She touched the hearts of all of her students through her dancing.

That night of March 21 changed our lives, though. Not only Rebecca's life, but also our whole family's. I will never forget when I first learned about this. My wife told me. I was working the night shift at the post office when Marian called me. Rebecca called her mom first. Then Marian called me and told me what happened. I couldn't speak. It was tragic. I knew that this would affect my family for the rest of their lives.

I immediately went home. Nobody was there. Jamie – that's Gina's boyfriend – and Marian went down to meet Rebecca and get her car. I was at the house when Marian and Jamie got back. Rebecca was with them. She looked awful. Tear-streaked face. I tried to hold her. She was limp. She felt so frail.

We were all sitting in the house, and that's when Rebecca and I found out that two children had died. When Jamie told Rebecca she broke down. She balled up in a fetal position and cried. She was afraid and said that she should have been the one to die. She wanted to go back to the scene of the accident. I told her not to go back. She tried to get up and leave the house but I grabbed her and stopped her. She was crazy out of her head with grief and I didn't think she could even drive. When I first found out about the accident, I wanted Rebecca to go back and turn herself in, I really did, but it was too late now and I didn't know what to do. I just knew I wanted to keep Rebecca safe and do the right thing for those kids and I couldn't see how I could do both. I wanted to protect my baby and I thought that more than anything else we needed to talk with a lawyer before we did anything else. We needed to think through this and

figure out what to do. It was late, I think sometime after midnight. If we could all just get through the night, then I would figure out who to call to make things better. I planned to do it in the morning.

Rebecca's car was still in the driveway, her 20XX-5 Toyota Echo. I guess my wife drove it to the house. I went to look at the car.

The hood and bumper on the driver's side were damaged—part of the bumper was torn off The windshield was cracked. The driver's side airbag had deployed. The front end had blood... and...other stuff...I don't know...blood...lots of it... all over the front end of the car. Horrible. I almost passed out from seeing it. I decided we needed to move it into the garage, we just couldn't leave it out in the driveway.

The garage hadn't been used as a dance studio for years; it was mainly just storage. It hdl the the car fine. After Jamie drove the car into the garage, I used the hose, Lysol and paper towels to clean the blood and other stuff off the car. I also wiped away blood from the driver-side windshield and door. There was a handprint on the left rear window, like someone had been beating on it. I threw everything out—even the Lysol can—in a black garbage bag. I wasn't sure what to do with it so I placed it in the garbage cans in the garage, then took the cans to the curb. Initially, no one except Steve really ever asked me about the location of the stuff I used to clean the car. Not even the police. I actually kind of forgot about it—with all that was going on—I guess the garbage collectors picked it up. They pick up on Fridays. By the time I was asked about it at deposition, well, it was gone. I don't know if they ever found it. It never came up at trial.

Man, that was a rough night. Rebecca was suicidal. I was really concerned. But we made it through the night, and the next morning, I told the family to stick to their normal schedule until I found a lawyer. I don't know if that was the right thing to do, but I didn't know what else to do. We needed to talk to a lawyer. We needed to figure out what we should do.

It was hard to know what to do. It was hard to know what happened. I don't think Rebecca even knew what happened. Rebecca never told me she hit any kids; she told me a body flew into her windshield. Because this was not her usual route home, I asked her if she saw anyone in the street, crossing the street. "Suitcase City"—that's the area she was in—is not a great neighborhood. What I mean to say is-- I mean, well, she just usually takes the interstate home. I don't feel comfortable with her driving in that part of town.

Rebecca said the first time she saw the body is when it flew into her windshield. The body could have been thrown into the windshield, I don't really know. It's not like we were trying to hide the truth. We weren't trying to hide anything from anyone. We just didn't know exactly what happened. And I don't think Rebecca is responsible for the death of those two boys. I will go to my grave saying that. I don't want to speak ill of anyone, but those children should not have been out on a street like that by themselves - it just isn't right.

The family did go about their business, though. They stuck to their normal schedules. I told them we should. Rebecca even taught school that Thursday. Somehow we all made it through the day after the accident. I think it was that night, Thursday night, we went to Marian's

parents' house in Pelican Bay. Everyone went, including the dogs. We moved in temporarily and tried to figure out what to do next.

I called Steve Levine on Friday. I'm so glad that I did. He really seemed to understand our pain, our fears. He didn't have to help us, you know. He didn't have to help my daughter. He didn't have to take this case. But he did. He really helped us figure out what we needed to do to straighten out this mess.

Levine knew what to do. Both he and Rebecca knew that she had to tell the police what happened. Levine knew we needed to try to visit the family. On Saturday Levine drove us to Mrs. Washington's home so that we could tell her how deeply sorry we were about this terrible tragedy. It wasn't the right time though. Mrs. Washington still needed time.

We stayed at Marian's parents until the news conference on Monday morning at 10 a.m. in Levine's office. We were finally able to come forward. Finally, Rebecca could tell Mrs. Washington and everyone how truly sorry she was for Mrs. Washington loss. Finally, Mrs. Washington could know that her family is in our thoughts and prayers.

BH Page 3 of 3.

Signed: Bill Hartwell
March 28, 20XX-2

Witnessed by: Detective Edwin Morris

Signed, Edwin Morris

March 28, 20XX-2

Exhibit 15

My name is Marian C. Hartwell. I am a teacher's aid at Lake Cypress Elementary School in Pelican Bay. I'm married to Bill Hartwell, and we live in Pelican Bay, Calusa County, FL. We have two daughters, Rebecca, 28, and Gina, 23.

My family moved to Florida from Cuba when I was just a little girl. I met Bill here and we have raised both of our daughters here in Calusa County. We are a very close family. Both of my daughters are wonderful people and very smart. We taught them to speak Spanish and that was their only language until they began school. Rebecca learned to speak English very well after she began pre-school. She was an excellent student. She attended Most Holy Redeemer Elementary School and then Riverridge High School where she always made 'A's and 'B's.

Both of my daughters were constantly dancing as children. They both loved to dance and took their dance classes very seriously. Rebecca began ballet around age 8. Bill converted the garage into a dance studio so that the girls could practice at home. Rebecca received a bachelor's degree in dance education from the University of South Florida. She is now a dance teacher at Northside Elementary School and she owns her own dance studio, The Dance, Dance, Dance Studio of Pelican Bay. All of her students really look up to her and admire her. Rebecca touches people through her love of dance.

March 21st was a horrible night that changed the lives of everyone in this family. Rebecca called me after the accident. She was sobbing and tried to explain to me what happened. Rebecca told me that a body had hit her windshield and that it was about to crack open. I told Rebecca to continue on towards the dance studio and to stay there. The studio was closer to Rebecca than our house and I didn't think that Rebecca should be driving because she was so upset. Bill was working the night shift at the post office. I had to call him to break the news. Bill wanted Rebecca to turn around and turn herself in. But when Rebecca called back she told me that she could not do that. I think she was just too upset. She was crying so hard, I could barely understand her. She wasn't making any sense. I think she was just too scared to go back, scared of what she would see.

After I spoke with my husband, I went with Gina's boyfriend Jamie to meet Rebecca and get her car. We drove by the scene of the accident first. We saw the ambulances and the sheriff's cruisers. I noticed a man standing in the street and I asked him what happened. He told me that a man had hit four children and that two of them were dead. I just started to cry. I couldn't believe that two children were gone. I felt some relief that this man was telling me a man had hit the children.

Rebecca kept calling me. She had arrived at the dance studio and was panicked. She told me that she was going to go to Publix and take all the pills she could. I told Jamie to get there as fast he could. We found the car that Rebecca was driving in the back of the studio. I went inside and found Rebecca alone, trembling. She was in shock. I put my jacket around her, helped her to the car that Jamie was driving, and I drove her car home.

When we got back to the house, Bill was home. We all sat in the house and just waited. Jamie broke the news to Rebecca that two of the children that had been hit had died. Rebecca just fell apart when she heard the news, curling up in a ball and just sobbing. She was so scared and said that she should have been the one to die. She kept saying, "I want to die." I want to die."

Later, Rebecca said that she wanted to go back to the scene of the accident, but Bill told her not to. She stopped talking. She wouldn't eat. We were so worried. Bill and I decided that the only way we could help and protect Rebecca at this point was to hire a lawyer. It was after midnight, so we decided that we would wait until morning and then make some calls. It was a long night for the whole family. Rebecca was suicidal and we needed to stay with her to keep her safe. The next morning, Bill told me and the girls that we were to follow our normal routine. We all followed Bill' order. I went to work. Rebecca even taught school that day. She called me once that day and told me that she couldn't take it and that she wanted to turn herself in.

I knew how Bill felt about this, so I told her to finish her day at work. Thursday night, the whole family stayed with my parents at their home in Tampa. We even took the dogs with us. We decided to stay there temporarily. It was comforting to be around family while we decided what to do next. On Friday, Bill called Steve Levine. He is the best lawyer in town. Steve was able to take the case and assud us that he could help Rebecca. I knew Steve was going to help us straighten everything out.

Steve decided that he and Rebecca would tell the police what happened. He also thought that Rebecca should visit the family of the children that had been hit. That Saturday, Steve drove us to the home of Mrs. Washington. The car ride was silent. We were all so nervous. We were going to explain to her how terribly sorry Rebecca was, we all were. We were met at the door by a friend of the family who explained that this was simply not the right time.

The whole family stayed with my parents until the news conference was held on Monday morning. It was at 10am at Steve's office. It was then that Rebecca was able to come forward and explain how sorry she was to everyone. Steve explained Rebecca's side of the story and let Rebecca apologize to Mrs. Washington.

Rebecca never tried to explain to us what happened. But she never said that she hit

anyone, either. She did say that a body flew into her windshield. Bill asked her if she had seen anyone trying to cross the street and Rebecca said that the first time she saw anyone was when the body hit her windshield. She kept saying, “No. No. No. I don’t know. No.” She was never a perfect driver, but I believe Rebecca. I believe that she did not hit those children.

I don’t want to say anything bad about anybody else, but really, how could you let your babies walk around like that in the dark? It just can’t be believed that something like that could happen this way. It just breaks my heart for those little ones. Nobody deserves to lose their babies, even folks that don’t work to pay for them. I don’t want to lose my baby to jail either. What good would that do for anyone?

MH Page 3 of 3.

Signed: Marian Hartwell

March 28, 20XX-2

Witnessed by: Detective Edwin Morris

Signed, Edwin Morris

March 28, 20XX-2

MB Page 1 of 2

Exhibit 16

My name is Matt Bader. I am 25 years old. I live at 715 Bower Avenue in Pelican Bay, Florida. On Wednesday, March 21st, 20XX-2 I was at a neighborhood cookout in the park between 15th Avenue South and 14th Avenue South; off 39th Street. After dinner and a few beers I played basketball with a bunch of other guys from the neighborhood. There was a pretty good size crowd watching us with a lot of kids and adults. When I went to get another drink, I looked at my watch. I noticed that it was about 10 minutes after 7:00 pm. The sun had set about 15 minutes before that, but it was still light enough to play basketball. As I was finishing my drink, I saw a few of the kids leaving the park headed to their home.

I recognized the kids as living on the other side of 39th Street. There was an older kid; I can't remember his name, carrying a younger kid. There were also two other smaller kids walking next to him. I think that they were his brothers and sisters. I remember that they were all holding hands as they walked back to their house. When they began to cross 39th Street, between 15th Avenue South and 14th Avenue South, I noticed that a few of the streetlights were not working. I believe that about six of them were out. While I was standing there, I wondered when those lights were ever going to get fixed.

I happened to look south when the kids began to cross the street. As soon as the kids stepped off the curb into 39th Street, I saw a dark car speeding towards them. It was painted a dark color and looked like a Honda Civic or a Toyota from the early 1990's or the late 1980's. I know the speed limit there was 30 miles per hour but that car was going much faster, like 45 miles per hour or so. I tried to yell but the kids couldn't hear me. I began to run to where the kids were, but there was nothing I could do; it happened so fast. I wish I could change what happened.

The dark car plowed into the kids. First the car hit the older boy carrying his younger brother or sister with a loud slapping or smacking sound. The little kid went flying off into the air. The older boy hit the front of the car's grill and seemed to roll up onto its hood and then smash into the car's front windshield before ending up in the intersection. Those kids were all holding hands! After the car hit the older boy carrying his younger brother or sister, the car also hit the two other kids. It was sick! One of them was knocked out of the way but the other. It was terrible, the other kid seemed to get caught under the car and dragged about half a block before tumbling out from under the car around 14th Avenue South. It happened so fast. The slapping or smacking sound was so loud that everyone in the park heard it and came running.

The car's driver must have known what happened because the dark car that hit the kids stopped for a few seconds. Then the driver turned the cars outside headlights lights off. There were no lights inside the car. I saw a dark shape but could not make out any details. The car's window's also looked like they were tinted. The car must have had a manual transmission because when the car's lights went out, I heard some grinding sounds; like shifting gears. The driver rapidly shifted gears and gunned the engine. Then the car took off, faster than it had been going

before it hit the kids. That driver must have known that something bad happened because it hit at least three of the kids directly. Afterwards, the car stopped for a few seconds before I heard the gears grinding as the driver made a quick getaway. I remember seeing lots of kid's shoes in the street and a puddle of blood. It happened so fast I didn't even think to look at the license plate.

Almost immediately after the car going northbound on 39th Street hit those kids, a van, coming southbound hit the two kids that were walking together that were knocked into the van's way by the car. I got a good look at the outside of the van. The van was white and looked like a Ford Econoline Van. There was a ladder on top. I noticed that the van did not seem to be going that fast. It appeared to be going the speed limit and was not going nearly as fast as the car was. I couldn't really see the driver clearly, but it did not look like the Van's driver could even see the kids. After hitting one of the kids the van stopped briefly and then left. What the car's driver did was sick. I don't' understand why the car's driver didn't stop. I hope they catch that driver. I also hope that someone learns something from this tragedy and fixes the streetlights and puts in some speed bumps! I brought in my cell phone. It has two videos taken that night. Both were emailed to me by someone else who must have been there that night. I don't know who took them but they sure look accurate to me.

I affirm that the foregoing statement was provided of my free will and that I was under no duress. This statement reflects my complete and total recollection of the events that occurred on 21 March 20XX-2.

MH Page 2 of 2.

Signed: Matthew Bader

July 7, 20XX-2

Witnessed by: Detective Edwin Morris

Signed, Edwin Morris

July 7, 20XX-2

16 - Movie 1 from Bader Cell Phone

00:00

Exhibit 17

Exhibit 18

MP3 File of 911 Call

- Please download and listen to the MP3 file for the 911 call.
- Compare this file to the official transcript provided previously

Exhibit 19

JAR - Page 1 of 2.

Exhibit 16

My name is James Allen Record. I hereby swear under penalty of perjury that the following is a true and accurate recounting of all relevant events related to my involvement in this case. I have prepared this affidavit at the request of the prosecuting attorney in the case of *State v. Hartwell.* I am a Lieutenant at the Pelican Bay Police Department, where I have worked for 12 years. I am 34 years of age.

I am currently assigned to the patrol division. On March 21, 20XX-2, probably around 7:15 p.m., I received a radio dispatch to investigate a hit and run involving three children on 15th Avenue South and 39th Street. That area is a stretch of Pelican Bay that is notorious for its drug dealers, cramped living spaces, and abandoned buildings. It is not a good place and our department has a lot of trouble down there, particularly with gangs and drugs. I was the first responding officer to the scene. It took me less than three minutes to get there, but there were already crowds of people swarming 39th street. It was an ugly crowd scene and I spent at least 15 minutes getting people out of the accident area. They kept coming back.

When I got there I immediately saw plastic and metal car parts scattered in the road, and sneakers and sandals that had been knocked loose from feet. The first victim I found was an adolescent boy who was lying on the pavement near the center stripe. He wasn't moving and his head and mouth were bleeding. The second victim, a little girl, was a few feet way from the boy. She was badly hurt with a broken leg, but she was talking.

Nobody could be sure how many bodies there were. Farther up the street, people were yelling, "there's another one up here!" I made my way through the crowd to the third victim; it was little boy, he couldn't have been more than 3 years old, and he wasn't moving. It appeared as though the boy was dragged about 150 feet by the vehicle that had hit him.

A tall man in the crowd found the fourth and smallest child. He was conscious, but it was impossible to tell how badly he was hurt because some of the streetlights were not working along that section of the road.

Three ambulances and a rescue chopper rushed the children to a local hospital and after they cleared the scene, a few other deputies and I started taping off the scene. We had to push back the crowd several times in an effort to preserve and mark the scattered evidence. We marked plastic car parts, metal car parts, sneakers, and sandals. We didn't really know what we were looking for or what would be important, there was so much debris. The most promising piece of evidence was a piece of black fender molding. On the inside, it said: T O Y O T A. I also found what appeared to be a hubcap from a Honda Accord. I could not tell how long the hubcap had been there but it was laying by the side of the road across the street from where the children were hit, near the Royal Garden Apartments.

As the crime scene technicians collected the marked evidence, I took several witnesses aside to give statements. A boy, about 16 years old, said that he remembered sitting on the bench when he saw a white van speeding, then he heard a loud boom. A 13-year-old remembered the children

standing on the grass between the sidewalk and the road. They were holding hands, as if they were about to cross the street. Then a few seconds later, the teen saw the children tumbling over a white van like dominoes.

Unfortunately, most of the statements were full of inconsistencies. Several witnesses said two vehicles were involved and a few said that three were involved. According to one person, a Honda had dragged a child down the street before flipping off its lights and speeding away. We had a difficult time getting a solid description of the vehicles. People did not agree on the models or their makes, which direction they were traveling, which ones had actually struck the children. No one got a license plate number.

As best I could tell, a car driving north on 39th Street - described as a late 1980s or early 1990s Honda Civic or a Toyota with tinted windows - was the first to strike the children. Then a second vehicle, traveling south - described as a white Ford Econoline van with a work ladder on top - hit them. JAR - Page 2 of 2.

James Alen Record

James Allen Record
July 13, 20XX-2

-*Notes*-

Calusa County Courier

Calusa County, Florida Tuesday, March 27, 20XX-2

Children Killed, School Teacher Comes Forward

Teacher casts blame on mother

By Suzie Slander

Yesterday a driver finally came forward in the tragic fatal accident that killed two children, ages 14 and 3, last Wednesday night at the intersection of 15th Avenue and 39th Street. The driver, Rebecca Hartwell, is a 28 year-old school teacher at Northside Elementary. She is also the owner-operator of the Dance, Dance, Dance Studio of Pelican Bay. Hartwell admitted that she was one of the drivers at the scene, but denied fault. Hartwell, surrounded by family and her lawyer, read a prepared statement yesterday at a press conference. Afterwards, in response to questions, Hartwell claimed that the children were "thrown into [her] car after being hit by another vehicle." Some witnesses claim Hartwell hit the children and then, with the 3 year old wedged under her car, drove another 150 feet, turned off her lights, and then sped away. Hartwell attempted to explain why she left the scene with the following: "It was dark; I was scared; I knew I had not caused the accident." Hartwell also appeared to blame the mother of the children for the accident, alluding that the mother was unfit, either an alcoholic or drug abuser, and placed the children in danger by allowing them to cross such a busy street at night. Speculation continues to swirl surrounding the case. Some witnesses state that a van hit the children and others claim there was a third car involved. Police continue to investigate the tragic accident.

After her prepared statement and unexpected remarks, Rebecca Hartwell and her family left the press conference together, hand-in-hand. Further attempts to ask the Hartwell's questions were met by their attorney stating that they did not have any further comment at this time.

The accident scene where the Washington children died looks much different in the light of day.

Jimmy Jones, CCC Photographer

Have you seen this van, or a van like it on 39th street the evening of March 21, 200XX-2? If so please call Crime Stoppers at 1-866-555-1234.

Pelican Bay Star Editorials
"Where People Talk"

Dear Ms. Washington and Citizens of Calusa County,

It is with my deepest sympathy that I come to you today. My heart goes out to Ms. Washington. My heart goes out to her children. And my heart goes out to our community.

To Ms. Washington, I can only say this--I cannot even begin to imagine the pain of losing a child, let alone two children. No one should have to go through that level of sorrow. I pray to God that you find peace during this difficult time.

To her surviving children, I pray that you are able to find comfort, as well as a safe environment to grow and live. To Jordan and Ronald, I pray your souls rest in peace.

To the community of Pelican Bay and Calusa Couty: I grieve with you. It was horrific, tragic, and senseless. I too cannot understand, for the life of me, why those four young children were left alone in such a neighborhood, at night, to cross a busy poorly lit street. The children were left to fend for themselves, and no children deserve that type of treatment; no children should be forced into that type of danger. I do not know if drugs or alcohol were involved, but those children should not have been left alone. That type of irresponsible conduct saddens and infuriates me. If an adult had been with those children, this would not have happened.

I did not hit those children. They were thrown into my car after being hit by another vehicle. It was dark; I was scared; I knew I had not caused the accident. I left because I did not know what to do. I regret not reacting with more calm and clarity after the accident. But my concern for Ms. Washington, her children, and the community is what has brought me before you today. I plead to the driver of the vehicle that hit these children—please come forward. Please. Thank you.

Sincerely,

Rebecca Hartwell
Rebecca Hartwell

Note: The opinions and statements expressed by Ms. Hartwell in the above letter to the editor, which we have printed in its entirety, in no way reflects the positions or opinions of the Pelican Bay Star – the editors.*

Pelican Bay Star March 26, 20XX-2 E-1

My name is Charissa Washington and I am 29 years old. I go by the name Rissa. I was born in Georgia, but I moved to Florida when I was a baby. I have never been married but I am a good woman and great mother. I had my first child, Jordan, when I was 15. I always wanted to be a teacher, but when Jordan was born I was unable to stay in school. My father helped me raise Jordan, and I took odd jobs to make a living. After Jordan, I had another son, who is now 10 and is living with his father. Then, I had four more children, August, Ronald, Charles, and my baby Laquinta.

I was pregnant with my seventh child that horrible spring. I love my children very much, and I try to give them the best life I can. I always worried about them because we did not live in a good neighborhood. We didn't have much – we are always moving from place to place, but we always had each other and were a good family. I did have trouble with the Department of Children and Family Services, DCF, but that was all a misunderstanding about a bad boyfriend. As God is my witness I did not know that he beat his own children. The minute I found out he was gone. He never hurt my babies though, the only person that did that was Ms. Hartwell. I don't know what rumors you may have heard about me and drug use, but I am here to tell you right now that I have never, ever taken any kind of illegal drug – I don't even drink.

Wednesday, March 21st was the worst day of my life. The kids had just gotten home from school, and they wanted to go play at the park. I told them that it was getting cold and that I didn't want them to go, but Jordan really wanted to go. He told me to stop treating him like a baby. He is very good with the babies, and I knew that he would watch them, so I told said they could go because I thought it would be safe. I walked the kids to the park because I am always nervous about the traffic and cars on the street by my apartment. The park is over there by the basketball courts and the community center. I told them to stay there until I would be back to pick them up before dark. I went back home, never knowing that was the last time I would see two of my boys alive. I saw that it was getting dark, so I went get the kids from the park. That was when a neighbor ran up yelling, so I started to run towards my babies.

I ran, even though I was pregnant, up to where my children were lying on the ground. People around told me to step back, and that I should not look. I saw Jordan lying there on the ground, bleeding from his head and mouth. Then I heard August scream. It was the worst feeling that a mother could have. I felt helpless, watching my babies there on the street, but there was nothing to do until help arrived. I knelt on the roadside until the ambulance came.

When I got to the hospital, there was nothing to do but wait. When I saw the chaplain come up to me, I knew that it was bad. He told me that Ronald was dead. I do not remember what happened after that, I felt like I was sleep walking in a dream. I remember falling down onto the floor screaming for my babies and they were nowhere for me to find them. Somebody picked me up off the floor and gave me a pill to calm me down. I remember that my family got to the hospital a bit later. I didn't know how I would make it without my kids, and when my family came to the hospital I started crying, "What am I going to do without my babies?" They had not caught the person who hit my children, so I went on the news and pled for whoever did this to turn themselves in. I said that I had no hate in my heart, but that I had a hole that needed to be filled. I needed to know who did this.

Luckily, a man named Mitchell Ritchie heard about what happened and wanted to help, so he called me up and told me that he would bury my babies in caskets. I picked one out for Jordan, and Mr. Ritchie ordered one specially made for Ronald. I was so grateful for Mr. Ritchie's kindness. At the funeral, when I saw my babies lying in their caskets, I screamed. It did not look like Ronald's face lying there, and I will always be haunted by that image. I fell before the caskets and I cried, and then I kissed each of my babies on the cheek to say goodbye. I said, "Mama be home to see you after awhile."

That weekend after the accident, a lawyer drove Mr. and Mrs. Hartwell over to my house. They were the parents of the girl who hit my children. I couldn't believe that they would come over so soon, I was such a mess, I told them that I was in no condition to see them that night.

Later, on the news, Jennifer Hartwell, the girl who hit my babies, expressed her apology to me by reading it off a piece of paper. It did not seem sincere or heartfelt. She did not explain what happened, and she came off looking like a victim when I was the one who lost my babies. I didn't know what to do, and when I talked to my friends about it, they told me that Jennifer Hartwell's lawyer was some important powerful lawyer who knew judges, and that Jennifer would probably not have to go to jail. It just made me so angry that someone could do something like this and not have to go to jail. I figured since she had a lawyer I better get me one too, just in case justice wasn't done you know, no other reason.

Everyone was talking about how she would not have to go to jail because she was white. Some people just see me as just a black girl who lived in the 'hood with a whole bunch of kids and no daddy. That important lawyer vowed to protect Jennifer Hartwell, but who was there to protect my kids? My lawyer told me that she would not be charged with murder, and I didn't understand how this was possible – she killed my babies. I vowed to Jesus that if she didn't go to jail I was still going to make her pay, under the law if nothing else.

Later that summer, I had my baby, Heaven. I had been so upset and unable to eat that my baby only weighed 5 pounds when she was born. My lawyer tried to get me to get a tubal ligation, but I had a dream where Jordan told me not to do it, so I knew it wasn't the right time. My lawyer was not happy about that.

They told me that I was not guilty of child neglect, but I knew that already, I would never neglect my babies. But, I still felt guilty for that day. I was even losing my hair and I was so upset about it. I still wish every day that I had not let them go to the park that day.

In the spring of 20XX-1, I was able to move my family to a new house with money from a settlement with Pelican Bay Electric Co. A Jacksonville law firm helped me with that case. They are different lawyers from the one I have now for this suit. We are very happy in our new house, and we feel safe here. It has helped me move on, although I still hear my dead babies whispering to me, asking me to forgive. I just hope they can forgive me.

CW Page 3 of 3.

Signed: Charissa Washington

April 29, 200XX-2

Witnessed by: Private Investigator Dana Stubbs

Signed, Dana Stubbs

May 3, 20XX-1

RH page 3 of 3.

My name is Rebecca Hartwell and I am 28 years old. I live with my parents, Marian and Bill, and my sister Gina, 23, in Pelican Bay, Florida. I would say that I grew up in a close-knit, Catholic, family. My mother is a Cuban immigrant and both my sister and I grew up speaking Spanish until we started pre- school. I went to St. Mary's Elementary School and then Incarnation High School. I always loved school and generally did pretty well, usually getting A's and B's. I went on to get my bachelor's in dance education from the University of South Florida.

Even though I loved school, my true love was dancing, and this has been my passion since childhood. My father was even kind enough to convert our old garage into a mini dance studio for me. I was constantly dancing, and I think at times I took dancing even more seriously than anything else in my life.

Even though I do not have children of my own, I am around them and work with them every day. I work at Northside Elementary school, teaching dance to children in the community. And I love them. My kids make me want to get up early and go to work every day. I love to bring the joy of dance into the lives of children.

In addition to teaching dance at Muller Elementary, I also own and operate my own dance studio, The Dance, Dance, Dance Studio of Pelican Bay. My parents helped me get started and provided financial backing. Dancing has been such a positive outlet for me that I want to give all the children I teach the opportunity to discover dance and allow it to affect their lives. My dance studio is only about 5 miles from the University Community Center, if only I hadn't take that road that night.

The night of March 21st was a nightmare come to life. I left Northside late that night, around 7pm, because I was helping the art teacher with a project for the school dedication ceremony coming up later that week. It was already dark when I drove out of the school parking lot in my Toyota Echo and headed for home.

I didn't take my usual route home. I turned right down north onto 39th street near the University. Usually the traffic lights are in my favor at that time of night—I can get home a little faster that way. All of the lights ahead looked good. I remember that I could see the traffic lights really well because several of the street lights were out. It was that time of day when the sun finally goes down completely and it really gets dark.

Not long after making the turn onto 39th, I was startled by something crashing hard into my windshield. It was so loud. I hadn't seen anything. My first thought was what was that? Followed pretty quickly by a Hail Mary.

It seemed like a body, but I couldn't be sure. There was no chance for me to even slam on my brakes because the object crashed into my car and then flew off my windshield so quickly. it seemed that something had dropped from the sky onto my windshield. I can't remember much else immediately after that, except for someone screaming! I guess my adrenaline kicked in to "fight or flight"—the only thing my body would let me do was to keep driving down the road.

Something jarred me—I heard what sounded like cracking ice. This sent me back into reality. I couldn't stop shaking and I couldn't catch my breath. I stopped the car.

My windshield was literally shattering in front of my eyes. I called my mother. I tried to tell her that something had stuck my windshield and that it was badly cracked. I'm not sure if she really understood what I was saying because I was crying so hard. She told me that I should drive over to the dance studio because it was closer to where I was than our house.

When I got to the dance studio, my mother was there and so was my sister's boyfriend Jamie. I had parked my car behind the studio in its usual spot. I was still crying and shaking. My mom told me that I insisted that I wanted to immediately go back to the area where the accident happened. I know I couldn't have driven my car back to the site—it was too unsafe to drive again with the windshield in that condition. Mom says I told them that I couldn't believe this was happening and that I wanted them to take me to Publix so I could buy sleeping pills. All I wanted to do was to take all the sleeping pills I could. put me into Jamie's car and drove me to our house.

When we got back home my father was there waiting for us. He hugged me. I was numb. I wanted to die.

At some point, my parents and Jamie sat me down and told me that on their way to the studio they had driven past the scene of the accident on 39th St. My mother told me she spoke with a bystander who told her that a car had stuck several children in the street and that two of them had died. I completely fell apart. All I could think about was whether these were my kids from Northside. I rolled onto the floor into the fetal position and just cried uncontrollably. If I could have traded my life to have one of those children back, I would have.

I kept asking my parents to take me to the scene of the accident in their car. I needed to go back there and explain what happened. They were only looking out for my safety. They kept telling me that it wasn't a good idea in the state I was in to go back there. That it was dangerous. That I needed to rest.

I couldn't eat, sleep or even talk. My parents told me they were going to get a lawyer first thing in the morning. My mother sat up with me the entire night. The next morning, my father insisted that we continue our normal routine to get our minds off things. I went to work the next day. The whole day I could barely speak. I didn't tell anyone what had happened. All I kept thinking about was how much I wanted to go back to the scene. I even called my mother and told her how much I wanted to go back there and tell the police what had happened. Because my parents were going to hire an attorney, they told me I should wait until I got professional advice before doing anything.

That night, my entire family went to stay with my grandparents in Pelican Bay. I wasn't sleeping and frankly, I think I may have taken those sleeping pills if it wasn't for my entire family keeping watch over me. My parents even refused to answer investigators' questions and risked being held in contempt and sent to jail for me.

On Friday, my dad got in contact with Steve Levine, a criminal defense attorney. He told my family that he would be able to help me to get everything straightened out. Just as I hoped, as soon as I got in touch with Steve, I was able to go to the police and tell them everything that had happened. I also told Steve that I wanted to visit Ms. Washington, the mother of the children who had been hit. I wanted to tell her how very truly sorry I was for her loss and that her children were in my prayers.

Unfortunately, when we arrived at the door we were met by a friend of the family who told us that Ms. Washington wasn't ready to speak with me at that time.

I went to confession on Sunday. I felt so horrible. I told Father Michaels everything. He was kind. Understanding. He did not judge me and did not give me extraordinary penance. He told me to be gentle with myself—that I needed to be still in order to hear God's counsel. That God would guide me and Mr. Levine. That He would forgive me.

That Monday, Mr. Steve Levine and I held a press conference. I had written a letter explaining how and why I was coming forward and how very sorry I was for Ms. Washington' loss. I was able to read this letter with the hope that Ms. Washington would hear it and understand what had happened. I wanted her to know that I wasn't a heartless, thoughtless person. I love children. I work with them every day and I love inspiring and teaching them. I got scared and let her fear get the best of me. I wish I could have been more level-headed and calm when the accident happened. The night of March 21st was a nightmare, one I've been reliving every day since then.

RH page 3 of 3.

Signed: Rebecca Hartwell

April 29, 20XX-2

Witnessed by: Private Investigator

Signed, Dana Stubbs

May 4, 20XX-1

State of XXXXX
UNIFORM COMMITMENT TO CUSTODY
OF DEPARTMENT OF CORRECTIONS

THE CIRCUIT COURT OF CALUSA COUNTY, IN THE SPRING TERM of 20XX-4
IN THE CASE OF:

STATE OF XXXXX CASE ID : 00XX(-4)1308 DIVISION: D
VS
DEFENDANT : Merinov Dimitri
AKA(S) : Ivan

IN THE NAME AND BY AUTHORITY OF THE STATE OF XXXXX, TO THE SHERRIFF OF SAID COUNTY AND THE DEPARTMENT OF CORRECTIONS OF SAID STATE, GREETING:

THE ABOVE NAMED DEFENDANT HAVING BEEN DULY CHARGED WITH THE OFFENSE SPECIFIED HEREIN IN THE ABOVE STYLED COURT, AND HAVING BEEN DULY CONVICTED AND ADJUDICATED GUILTY OF AND SENTENCE FOR SAID OFFENSE BY SAID COURT, AS APPEARS FROM THE ATTACHED CERTIFIED COPIES OF INFORMATION FILED JUDGMENT AND SENTENCE, AND FELONY DISPOSITION AND SENTENCE DATA FROM WHICH ARE HEREBY MADE PARTS HEROF;

NOW THEREFORE, THIS TO COMMAND YOU, THE SAID SHERIFF, TO TAKE AND KEEP, AND, WITHIN A REASONABLE TIME AFTER RECEIVING THIS COMMITMENT, SAFELY DELIVER THE SAID DEFENDANT, TOGETHER WITH ANY PERTINENT INVESTIGATION REPORT PREPARED IN THIS CASE, INTO THE CUSTODY OF THE DEPARTMENT OF CORRECTIONS OF THE STATE OF XXXXX: AND THIS IS TO COMMAND YOU, THE SAID DEPARTMENT OF CORRECTIONS, BY AND THROUGH YOUR SECRETARY, REGIONAL DIRECTORS, SUPERINTENDANTS, AND OTHER OFFICIALS, TO KEEP AND SAFELY IMPRISON THE SAID DEFENDANT FRO THE TERM OF SAID SENTENCE IN THE INSTITUTION IN THE STATE CORRECTIONAL SYSTEM TO WHICH YOU, THE SAID DEPARTMENT OF CORRECTIONS, MAY CAUSE THE SAID DEFENDANT TO BE CONVEYED OR THEREAFTER TRANSFERRED. AND THESE PRESENTS SHALL BE YOUR AUTHORITY FOR THE SAME. HEREIN NOT FAIL

WITNESS THE HONORABLE JEREMY PARKER
JUDGE OF THE SAID COURT, AS ALSO CONNIE EVANS
CLERK, AND THE SEAL THEREOF, THIS
14th DAY OF February 20XX-4

BY: Margaret Mills
DEPUTY CLERK

IN THE FIRST JUDICIAL CIRCUIT IN AND FOR
CALUSA COUNTY, STATE OF XXXXX

CIRCUIT CRIMINAL DIVISON

STATE OF XXXXX
v.
DIMITRI MERINOV
DEFENDANT

DIVISION: D

CASE NUMBER: 00XX(-4)1308

CERTIFICATE OF SERVICE

I, Connie Evans, Clerk of the Circuit Court of the County of Calusa, State of XXXXX, having by law the custody of the seal and all records, books, documents and papers of or appertaining to the Circuit Court, do hereby certify that a true and correct copy of the Judgment and Sentence has been hand delivered to the State Attorney and mailed to the Defense Attorney.

IN WITNESS WHEREOF, I have hereunto set my hand and seal of said Circuit Court, this 14th day of February A.D. 20XX-4.

CONNIE EVANS
As Clerk of Circuit Court

Margaret Mills
As Deputy Clerk
Circuit Criminal Division

IN THE CIRCUIT COURT, 1ST JUDICIAL CIRCUIT
IN AND FOR CALUSA COUNTY, XXXXX
DIVISION : D
CASE NUMBER : 00XX(-4)1308

STATE OF XXXXX
VS
Dimitri Merinov
DEFENDANT

---------------------------------JUDGMENT--

THE DEFENDANT, Dimitri Merinov, BEING PERSONALLY BEFORE
THIS COURT REPRESENTED WITH
PRIVATE ATTORNEY
John Saunders, Esquire
THE ATTORNEY OF RECORD AND THE STATE REPRESENTED BY ASSISTANT STATE ATTORNEY
NICHOLAS COX, AND HAVING

Been tried and found guilty by a jury of the following crime(s): 3

COUNT	CRIME	STATUTE	COURT ACTION	DATE
1	~~LEWD OR LASCIVIOUS MOLESTATION~~	~~80004~~	NOT GUILTY	6 January 20XX-4
2	~~SEXUAL BATTERY~~	~~794011~~	NOT GUILTY	6 January 20XX-4
3	LEWD OR LASCIVIOUS EXHIBITION	800047	ADJG GUILTY	6 January 20XX-4

And no cause being shown why the defendant should not be adjudicated guilty, it is ordered that the defendant is hereby adjudicated guilty of the above crime(s).

AND PURSUANT TO SECTION 943.325, XXXXX STATUTES, HAVING BEEN CONFICTED OF ATTEMPTS OR OFFENSES RELATING TO SEXUAL BATTERY (CH. 794) OR LEWD AND LASCIVIOUS CONDUCT (CH. 800) THE DEFENDANT SHALL BE REQUIRED TO SUBMIT BLOOD SPECIMENS

DEFENDANT Dimitri Merinov

Division : D
Case Number : 00XX(-4)1308
OBTS Number : 12394872

----------SENTENCE----------

THE DEFENDANT, BEING PERSONALLY BEFORE THIS COURT, ACCOMPANIED BY THE DEFENDANT'S ATTORNEY OF RECORD, PRIVATE ATTORNEY John Saunders, Esquire
AND HAVING BEEN ADJUDGED GUILTY HEREIN, AND THE COURT HAVING BEEN GIVEN THE DEFENDANT AN OPPORTUNITY TO BE HEARD AND TO OFFER MATTERS IN MITIGATION OF SENTENCE, AND TO SHOW CAUSE WHY THE DEFENDANT SHOULD NOT BE SENTENCED AS PROVIDED BY LAW AND NO CAUSE BEING SHOWN

IT IS THE SENTENCE OF THIS COURT THAT THE DEFENDANT:

Pay a fine of $3000.00, pursuant to appropriate XXXXX Statutes.
Is hereby committed to the custody of the Department of Corrections for a term of: 3 Years

----------OTHER PROVISIONS----------

AS TO COUNT(S) : 3
THE FOLLOWING MANDATORY/MINIMUM PROVISIONS APPLY TO THE SENTENCE IMPOSED :

JAIL CREDIT: It is further ordered that the defendant shall be allowed a total of 223 DAYS as credit for time incarcerated before imposition of this sentence.

DEFENDANT Dimitri Merinov

Division : D
Case Number : 00XX(-4)1308
OBTS Number : 12394872

----------OTHER PROVISIONS----------

Sentencing guidelines filed.

IN THE EVEN THE ABOVE SENTENCE IS TO THE DEPARTMENT OF CORRECTIONS, THE SHERIFF OF CALUSA COUNTY, XXXXX, IS HEREBY ORDERED AND DIRECTED TO DELIVER THE DEFENDANT TO THE DEPARTMENT OF CORRECTIONS AT THE FACILITY DESIGNATED BY THE DEPARTMENT TOGETHER WITH A COPY OF THIS JUDGMENT AND SENTENCE AND ANY OTHER DOCUMENTS SPECIFIED BY XXXXX STATUTE
THE DEFENDANT IN OPEN COURT WAS ADVISED OF THE RIGHT TO APPEAL FROM THIS SENTENCE BY FILING NOTICE OF APPEAL WITHIN 30 DAYS FROM THIS DATE WITH THE CLERK OF THIS COURT AND THE DEFENDANT'S RIGHT TO THE ASSISTANCE OF COUNSEL IN TAKING THE APPEAL AT THE EXPENSE OF THE STATE SHOWIN OF INDIGENCY.
DONE AND ORDERED IN CALUSA COUNTY, XXXXX, THIS 14TH DAY OF February 20XX-4

State of XXXXX
UNIFORM COMMITMENT TO CUSTODY
OF DEPARTMENT OF CORRECTIONS

THE CIRCUIT COURT OF CALUSA COUNTY, IN THE SPRING TERM of 20XX-4
IN THE CASE OF:

STATE OF XXXXX CASE ID : 20XX(-3)1978 DIVISION: D
VS
DEFENDANT : Bader Matthew
AKA(S) : Nick

IN THE NAME AND BY AUTHORITY OF THE STATE OF XXXXX, TO THE SHERRIFF OF SAID COUNTY AND THE DEPARTMENT OF CORRECTIONS OF SAID STATE, GREETING:

THE ABOVE NAMED DEFENDANT HAVING BEEN DULY CHARGED WITH THE OFFENSE SPECIFIED HEREIN IN THE ABOVE STYLED COURT, AND HAVING BEEN DULY CONVICTED AND ADJUDICATED GUILTY OF AND SENTENCE FOR SAID OFFENSE BY SAID COURT, AS APPEARS FROM THE ATTACHED CERTIFIED COPIES OF INFORMATION FILED JUDGMENT AND SENTENCE, AND FELONY DISPOSITION AND SENTENCE DATA FROM WHICH ARE HEREBY MADE PARTS HEROF;

NOW THEREFORE, THIS TO COMMAND YOU, THE SAID SHERIFF, TO TAKE AND KEEP, AND, WITHIN A REASONABLE TIME AFTER RECEIVING THIS COMMITMENT, SAFELY DELIVER THE SAID DEFENDANT, TOGETHER WITH ANY PERTINENT INVESTIGATION REPORT PREPARED IN THIS CASE, INTO THE CUSTODY OF THE DEPARTMENT OF CORRECTIONS OF THE STATE OF XXXXX: AND THIS IS TO COMMAND YOU, THE SAID DEPARTMENT OF CORRECTIONS, BY AND THROUGH YOUR SECRETARY, REGIONAL DIRECTORS, SUPERINTENDANTS, AND OTHER OFFICIALS, TO KEEP AND SAFELY IMPRISON THE SAID DEFENDANT FRO THE TERM OF SAID SENTENCE IN THE INSTITUTION IN THE STATE CORRECTIONAL SYSTEM TO WHICH YOU, THE SAID DEPARTMENT OF CORRECTIONS, MAY CAUSE THE SAID DEFENDANT TO BE CONVEYED OR THEREAFTER TRANSFERRED. AND THESE PRESENTS SHALL BE YOUR AUTHORITY FOR THE SAME. HEREIN NOT FAIL

WITNESS THE HONORABLE JEREMY PARKER
JUDGE OF THE SAID COURT, AS ALSO CONNIE EVANS
CLERK, AND THE SEAL THEREOF, THIS
24th DAY OF JUNE 20XX-3

BY: Margaret Mills
DEPUTY CLERK

IN THE FIRST JUDICIAL CIRCUIT IN AND FOR
CALUSA COUNTY, STATE OF XXXXX

CIRCUIT CRIMINAL DIVISON

STATE OF XXXXX v. <u>MATTHEW BADER</u> DEFENDANT	DIVISION: D CASE NUMBER: 20XX(-3)1978

CERTIFICATE OF SERVICE

I, Connie Evans, Clerk of the Circuit Court of the County of Calusa, State of XXXXX, having by law the custody of the seal and all records, books, documents and papers of or appertaining to the Circuit Court, do hereby certify that a true and correct copy of the Judgment and Sentence has been hand delivered to the State Attorney and mailed to the Defense Attorney.

IN WITNESS WHEREOF, I have hereunto set my hand and seal of said Circuit Court, this 24th day of June A.D. 20XX-3.

CONNIE EVANS
As Clerk of Circuit Court

Margaret Mills
As Deputy Clerk
Circuit Criminal Division

IN THE CIRCUIT COURT, 1ST JUDICIAL CIRCUIT
IN AND FOR CALUSA COUNTY, XXXXX
DIVISION : D
CASE NUMBER : 20XX(-3)1978

STATE OF XXXXX
VS
Matthew Bader
DEFENDANT

----------------------------------JUDGMENT--

THE DEFENDANT, Matthew Bader, BEING PERSONALLY BEFORE
THIS COURT REPRESENTED WITH
PRIVATE ATTORNEY
Raymond Tillery, Esquire
THE ATTORNEY OF RECORD AND THE STATE REPRESENTED BY ASSISTANT STATE ATTORNEY
Lee Heller-Pearlman, AND HAVING

Been tried and found guilty by a jury of the following crime(s): 1

COUNT	CRIME	STATUTE	COURT ACTION	DATE
1	Possession of a Controlled Substance, to wit, COCAINE	80112	GUILTY	16 May 20XX-3

And no cause being shown why the defendant should not be adjudicated guilty, it is ordered that the defendant is hereby adjudicated guilty of the above crime(s).

DEFENDANT Matthew Bader

Division : D
Case Number : 20XX(-3)1978
OBTS Number : 23488721

SENTENCE

THE DEFENDANT, BEING PERSONALLY BEFORE THIS COURT, ACCOMPANIED BY THE DEFENDANT'S ATTORNEY OF RECORD, PRIVATE ATTORNEY Raymond Tillery, Esquire
AND HAVING BEEN ADJUDGED GUILTY HEREIN, AND THE COURT HAVING BEEN GIVEN THE DEFENDANT AN OPPORTUNITY TO BE HEARD AND TO OFFER MATTERS IN MITIGATION OF SENTENCE, AND TO SHOW CAUSE WHY THE DEFENDANT SHOULD NOT BE SENTENCED AS PROVIDED BY LAW AND NO CAUSE BEING SHOWN

IT IS THE SENTENCE OF THIS COURT THAT THE DEFENDANT:

Pay a fine of $500.00, pursuant to appropriate XXXXX Statutes.
Is hereby committed to the custody of the Department of Corrections for a term of: 1Year, 6 Months

OTHER PROVISIONS

AS TO COUNT(S) : 1
THE FOLLOWING MANDATORY/MINIMUM PROVISIONS APPLY TO THE SENTENCE IMPOSED :

JAIL CREDIT: It is further ordered that the defendant shall be allowed a total of 275 DAYS as credit for time incarcerated before imposition of this sentence.

DEFENDANT Matthew Bader

Division : D
Case Number : 20XX(-3)1978
OBTS Number : 23488721

OTHER PROVISIONS

Sentencing guidelines filed.

IN THE EVENT THE ABOVE SENTENCE IS TO THE DEPARTMENT OF CORRECTIONS, THE SHERIFF OF CALUSA COUNTY, XXXXX, IS HEREBY ORDERED AND DIRECTED TO DELIVER THE DEFENDANT TO THE DEPARTMENT OF CORRECTIONS AT THE FACILITY DESIGNATED BY THE DEPARTMENT TOGETHER WITH A COPY OF THIS JUDGMENT AND SENTENCE AND ANY OTHER DOCUMENTS SPECIFIED BY XXXXX STATUTE
THE DEFENDANT IN OPEN COURT WAS ADVISED OF THE RIGHT TO APPEAL FROM THIS SENTENCE BY FILING NOTICE OF APPEAL WITHIN 30 DAYS FROM THIS DATE WITH THE CLERK OF THIS COURT AND THE DEFENDANT'S RIGHT TO THE ASSISTANCE OF COUNSEL IN TAKING THE APPEAL AT THE EXPENSE OF THE STATE SHOWING OF INDIGENCY.
DONE AND ORDERED IN CALUSA COUNTY, XXXXX, THIS 24TH DAY OF June 20XX-3

State of XXXXX
UNIFORM COMMITMENT TO CUSTODY
OF DEPARTMENT OF CORRECTIONS

THE CIRCUIT COURT OF CALUSA COUNTY, IN THE SPRING TERM of 20XX-10
IN THE CASE OF:

STATE OF XXXXX CASE ID : 20XX(-11)1898 DIVISION: D
VS
DEFENDANT : Rebecca Hartwell
AKA(S) :

IN THE NAME AND BY AUTHORITY OF THE STATE OF XXXXX, TO THE SHERRIFF OF SAID COUNTY AND THE DEPARTMENT OF CORRECTIONS OF SAID STATE, GREETING:

THE ABOVE NAMED DEFENDANT HAVING BEEN DULY CHARGED WITH THE OFFENSE SPECIFIED HEREIN IN THE ABOVE STYLED COURT, AND HAVING BEEN DULY CONVICTED AND ADJUDICATED GUILTY OF AND SENTENCE FOR SAID OFFENSE BY SAID COURT, AS APPEARS FROM THE ATTACHED CERTIFIED COPIES OF INFORMATION FILED JUDGMENT AND SENTENCE, AND FELONY DISPOSITION AND SENTENCE DATA FROM WHICH ARE HEREBY MADE PARTS HEROF;

NOW THEREFORE, THIS TO COMMAND YOU, THE SAID SHERIFF, TO TAKE AND KEEP, AND, WITHIN A REASONABLE TIME AFTER RECEIVING THIS COMMITMENT, SAFELY DELIVER THE SAID DEFENDANT, TOGETHER WITH ANY PERTINENT INVESTIGATION REPORT PREPARED IN THIS CASE, INTO THE CUSTODY OF THE DEPARTMENT OF CORRECTIONS OF THE STATE OF XXXXX: AND THIS IS TO COMMAND YOU, THE SAID DEPARTMENT OF CORRECTIONS, BY AND THROUGH YOUR SECRETARY, REGIONAL DIRECTORS, SUPERINTENDANTS, AND OTHER OFFICIALS, TO KEEP AND SAFELY IMPRISON THE SAID DEFENDANT FRO THE TERM OF SAID SENTENCE IN THE INSTITUTION IN THE STATE CORRECTIONAL SYSTEM TO WHICH YOU, THE SAID DEPARTMENT OF CORRECTIONS, MAY CAUSE THE SAID DEFENDANT TO BE CONVEYED OR THEREAFTER TRANSFERRED. AND THESE PRESENTS SHALL BE YOUR AUTHORITY FOR THE SAME. HEREIN NOT FAIL

WITNESS THE HONORABLE JEREMY PARKER
JUDGE OF THE SAID COURT, AS ALSO CONNIE EVANS
CLERK, AND THE SEAL THEREOF, THIS
21st DAY OF January 20XX-10

BY: Margaret Mills
DEPUTY CLERK

IN THE FIRST JUDICIAL CIRCUIT IN AND FOR
CALUSA COUNTY, STATE OF XXXXX

CIRCUIT CRIMINAL DIVISON

STATE OF XXXXX
v.
Rebecca Hartwell
DEFENDANT

DIVISION: D

CASE NUMBER: 20XX(-11)1898

CERTIFICATE OF SERVICE

I, Connie Evans, Clerk of the Circuit Court of the County of Calusa, State of XXXXX, having by law the custody of the seal and all records, books, documents and papers of or appertaining to the Circuit Court, do hereby certify that a true and correct copy of the Judgment and Sentence has been hand delivered to the State Attorney and mailed to the Defense Attorney.

IN WITNESS WHEREOF, I have hereunto set my hand and seal of said Circuit Court, this 21st day of January A.D. 20XX-10.

CONNIE EVANS
As Clerk of Circuit Court

Margaret Mills

As Deputy Clerk
Circuit Criminal Division

IN THE CIRCUIT COURT, 1ST JUDICIAL CIRCUIT
IN AND FOR CALUSA COUNTY, XXXXX
DIVISION : D
CASE NUMBER : 20XX(-11)1898

STATE OF XXXXX
VS
Rebecca Hartwell
DEFENDANT

----------------------------------JUDGMENT--

THE DEFENDANT, Rebecca Hartwell, BEING PERSONALLY BEFORE THIS COURT REPRESENTED WITH PRIVATE ATTORNEY
John Head, Esquire
THE ATTORNEY OF RECORD AND THE STATE REPRESENTED BY ASSISTANT STATE ATTORNEY George Peabody Smalley, AND HAVING

Been tried and found guilty by a jury of the following crime(s): 1

COUNT	CRIME	STATUTE	COURT ACTION	DATE
1	Reckless Driving	80120	GUILTY	13 Dec 20XX-11

And no cause being shown why the defendant should not be adjudicated guilty, it is ordered that the defendant is hereby adjudicated guilty of the above crime(s).

DEFENDANT Rebecca Hartwell

Division : D
Case Number : 20XX(-11)1898
OBTS Number : 32323496

------------------------------------SENTENCE------------------------------------

THE DEFENDANT, BEING PERSONALLY BEFORE THIS COURT, ACCOMPANIED BY THE DEFENDANT'S ATTORNEY OF RECORD, PRIVATE ATTORNEY John Head, Esquire
AND HAVING BEEN ADJUDGED GUILTY HEREIN, AND THE COURT HAVING BEEN GIVEN THE DEFENDANT AN OPPORTUNITY TO BE HEARD AND TO OFFER MATTERS IN MITIGATION OF SENTENCE, AND TO SHOW CAUSE WHY THE DEFENDANT SHOULD NOT BE SENTENCED AS PROVIDED BY LAW AND NO CAUSE BEING SHOWN

IT IS THE SENTENCE OF THIS COURT THAT THE DEFENDANT:

Pay a fine of $1500.00, pursuant to appropriate XXXXX Statutes.
Is hereby committed to the custody of the Department of Corrections for a term of: 24 Months, 18 months of said sentence to be suspended pending successful completion of 4 years probation.

--------------------------------OTHER PROVISIONS--------------------------------

AS TO COUNT(S) : 1
THE FOLLOWING MANDATORY/MINIMUM PROVISIONS APPLY TO THE SENTENCE IMPOSED :

None

DEFENDANT Rebecca Hartwell

Division : D
Case Number : 20XX(-11)1898
OBTS Number : 32323497

--------------------------------OTHER PROVISIONS--------------------------------

Sentencing guidelines filed.

IN THE EVENT THE ABOVE SENTENCE IS TO THE DEPARTMENT OF CORRECTIONS, THE SHERIFF OF CALUSA COUNTY, XXXXX, IS HEREBY ORDERED AND DIRECTED TO DELIVER THE DEFENDANT TO THE DEPARTMENT OF CORRECTIONS AT THE FACILITY DESIGNATED BY THE DEPARTMENT TOGETHER WITH A COPY OF THIS JUDGMENT AND SENTENCE AND ANY OTHER DOCUMENTS SPECIFIED BY XXXXX STATUTE
THE DEFENDANT IN OPEN COURT WAS ADVISED OF THE RIGHT TO APPEAL FROM THIS SENTENCE BY FILING NOTICE OF APPEAL WITHIN 30 DAYS FROM THIS DATE WITH THE CLERK OF THIS COURT AND THE DEFENDANT'S RIGHT TO THE ASSISTANCE OF COUNSEL IN TAKING THE APPEAL AT THE EXPENSE OF THE STATE SHOWIN OF INDIGENCY.
DONE AND ORDERED IN CALUSA COUNTY, XXXXX, THIS 21st DAY OF January 20XX-10

State of XXXXX
UNIFORM COMMITMENT TO CUSTODY
OF DEPARTMENT OF CORRECTIONS

THE CIRCUIT COURT OF CALUSA COUNTY, IN THE SPRING TERM of 20XX-4
IN THE CASE OF:

STATE OF XXXXX CASE ID : 20XX(-5)1918 DIVISION: D
v.
DEFENDANT : Charissa Washington
AKA(S) : Rissa

IN THE NAME AND BY AUTHORITY OF THE STATE OF XXXXX, TO THE SHERRIFF OF SAID COUNTY AND THE DEPARTMENT OF CORRECTIONS OF SAID STATE, GREETING:

THE ABOVE NAMED DEFENDANT HAVING BEEN DULY CHARGED WITH THE OFFENSE SPECIFIED HEREIN IN THE ABOVE STYLED COURT, AND HAVING BEEN DULY CONVICTED AND ADJUDICATED GUILTY OF AND SENTENCE FOR SAID OFFENSE BY SAID COURT, AS APPEARS FROM THE ATTACHED CERTIFIED COPIES OF INFORMATION FILED JUDGMENT AND SENTENCE, AND FELONY DISPOSITION AND SENTENCE DATA FROM WHICH ARE HEREBY MADE PARTS HEROF;

NOW THEREFORE, THIS TO COMMAND YOU, THE SAID SHERIFF, TO TAKE AND KEEP, AND, WITHIN A REASONABLE TIME AFTER RECEIVING THIS COMMITMENT, SAFELY DELIVER THE SAID DEFENDANT, TOGETHER WITH ANY PERTINENT INVESTIGATION REPORT PREPARED IN THIS CASE, INTO THE CUSTODY OF THE DEPARTMENT OF CORRECTIONS OF THE STATE OF XXXXX: AND THIS IS TO COMMAND YOU, THE SAID DEPARTMENT OF CORRECTIONS, BY AND THROUGH YOUR SECRETARY, REGIONAL DIRECTORS, SUPERINTENDANTS, AND OTHER OFFICIALS, TO KEEP AND SAFELY IMPRISON THE SAID DEFENDANT FRO THE TERM OF SAID SENTENCE IN THE INSTITUTION IN THE STATE CORRECTIONAL SYSTEM TO WHICH YOU, THE SAID DEPARTMENT OF CORRECTIONS, MAY CAUSE THE SAID DEFENDANT TO BE CONVEYED OR THEREAFTER TRANSFERRED. AND THESE PRESENTS SHALL BE YOUR AUTHORITY FOR THE SAME. HEREIN NOT FAIL

WITNESS THE HONORABLE JEREMY PARKER
JUDGE OF THE SAID COURT, AS ALSO CONNIE EVANS
CLERK, AND THE SEAL THEREOF, THIS
21st DAY OF April 20XX-4

BY: Margaret Mills
DEPUTY CLERK

IN THE FIRST JUDICIAL CIRCUIT IN AND FOR
CALUSA COUNTY, STATE OF XXXXX

CIRCUIT CRIMINAL DIVISON

STATE OF XXXXX
v.
Charissa Washington
DEFENDANT

DIVISION: D

CASE NUMBER: 20XX(-5)1918

CERTIFICATE OF SERVICE

I, Connie Evans, Clerk of the Circuit Court of the County of Calusa, State of XXXXX, having by law the custody of the seal and all records, books, documents and papers of or appertaining to the Circuit Court, do hereby certify that a true and correct copy of the Judgment and Sentence has been hand delivered to the State Attorney and mailed to the Defense Attorney.

IN WITNESS WHEREOF, I have hereunto set my hand and seal of said Circuit Court, this 21st day of April A.D. 20XX-4.

CONNIE EVANS
As Clerk of Circuit Court

Margaret Mills
As Deputy Clerk
Circuit Criminal Division

IN THE CIRCUIT COURT, 1ST JUDICIAL CIRCUIT
IN AND FOR CALUSA COUNTY, XXXXX
DIVISION : D
CASE NUMBER : 20XX(-5)1918

STATE OF XXXXX
v.
Charissa Washington
DEFENDANT

--------------------------------JUDGMENT--

THE DEFENDANT, Charissa Washington BEING PERSONALLY BEFORE
THIS COURT REPRESENTED WITH
PRIVATE ATTORNEY
Norm Pearson, Esquire
THE ATTORNEY OF RECORD AND THE STATE REPRESENTED BY ASSISTANT STATE ATTORNEY
George Peabody Smalley, AND HAVING

Been tried and found guilty by a jury of the following crime(s): 1

COUNT	CRIME	STATUTE	COURT ACTION	DATE
1	Filing a false police report	80107	GUILTY	21 April 20XX-4

And no cause being shown why the defendant should not be adjudicated guilty, it is ordered that the defendant is hereby adjudicated guilty of the above crime(s).

DEFENDANT Charissa Washington

Division : D
Case Number : 20XX(-5)1918
OBTS Number : 37624344

-----SENTENCE-----

THE DEFENDANT, BEING PERSONALLY BEFORE THIS COURT, ACCOMPANIED BY THE DEFENDANT'S ATTORNEY OF RECORD, PRIVATE ATTORNEY Norm Pearson, Esquire
AND HAVING BEEN ADJUDGED GUILTY HEREIN, AND THE COURT HAVING BEEN GIVEN THE DEFENDANT AN OPPORTUNITY TO BE HEARD AND TO OFFER MATTERS IN MITIGATION OF SENTENCE, AND TO SHOW CAUSE WHY THE DEFENDANT SHOULD NOT BE SENTENCED AS PROVIDED BY LAW AND NO CAUSE BEING SHOWN

IT IS THE SENTENCE OF THIS COURT THAT THE DEFENDANT:

Pay a fine of $1500.00, pursuant to appropriate XXXXX Statutes.
Is hereby committed to the custody of the Department of Corrections for a term of: 12 Months, sentence to be suspended pending successful completion of 4 years probation.

-----OTHER PROVISIONS-----

AS TO COUNT(S) : 1
THE FOLLOWING MANDATORY/MINIMUM PROVISIONS APPLY TO THE SENTENCE IMPOSED :

None

DEFENDANT Charissa Washington

Division : D
Case Number : 20XX(-5)1918
OBTS Number : 37624344

-----OTHER PROVISIONS-----

Sentencing guidelines filed.

IN THE EVENT THE ABOVE SENTENCE IS TO THE DEPARTMENT OF CORRECTIONS, THE SHERIFF OF CALUSA COUNTY, XXXXX, IS HEREBY ORDERED AND DIRECTED TO DELIVER THE DEFENDANT TO THE DEPARTMENT OF CORRECTIONS AT THE FACILITY DESIGNATED BY THE DEPARTMENT TOGETHER WITH A COPY OF THIS JUDGMENT AND SENTENCE AND ANY OTHER DOCUMENTS SPECIFIED BY XXXXX STATUTE
THE DEFENDANT IN OPEN COURT WAS ADVISED OF THE RIGHT TO APPEAL FROM THIS SENTENCE BY FILING NOTICE OF APPEAL WITHIN 30 DAYS FROM THIS DATE WITH THE CLERK OF THIS COURT AND THE DEFENDANT'S RIGHT TO THE ASSISTANCE OF COUNSEL IN TAKING THE APPEAL AT THE EXPENSE OF THE STATE SHOWIN OF INDIGENCY.
DONE AND ORDERED IN CALUSA COUNTY, XXXXX, THIS 21st DAY OF April 20XX-4

State of XXXXX
UNIFORM COMMITMENT TO CUSTODY
OF DEPARTMENT OF CORRECTIONS

THE CIRCUIT COURT OF CALUSA COUNTY, IN THE SPRING TERM of 20XX-8
IN THE CASE OF:

STATE OF XXXXX CASE ID : 20XX(-6)2132 DIVISION: D
VS
DEFENDANT : Charissa Washington
AKA(S) : Rissa

IN THE NAME AND BY AUTHORITY OF THE STATE OF XXXXX, TO THE SHERRIFF OF SAID COUNTY AND THE DEPARTMENT OF CORRECTIONS OF SAID STATE, GREETING:

THE ABOVE NAMED DEFENDANT HAVING BEEN DULY CHARGED WITH THE OFFENSE SPECIFIED HEREIN IN THE ABOVE STYLED COURT, AND HAVING BEEN DULY CONVICTED AND ADJUDICATED GUILTY OF AND SENTENCE FOR SAID OFFENSE BY SAID COURT, AS APPEARS FROM THE ATTACHED CERTIFIED COPIES OF INFORMATION FILED JUDGMENT AND SENTENCE, AND FELONY DISPOSITION AND SENTENCE DATA FROM WHICH ARE HEREBY MADE PARTS HEROF;

NOW THEREFORE, THIS TO COMMAND YOU, THE SAID SHERIFF, TO TAKE AND KEEP, AND, WITHIN A REASONABLE TIME AFTER RECEIVING THIS COMMITMENT, SAFELY DELIVER THE SAID DEFENDANT, TOGETHER WITH ANY PERTINENT INVESTIGATION REPORT PREPARED IN THIS CASE, INTO THE CUSTODY OF THE DEPARTMENT OF CORRECTIONS OF THE STATE OF XXXXX: AND THIS IS TO COMMAND YOU, THE SAID DEPARTMENT OF CORRECTIONS, BY AND THROUGH YOUR SECRETARY, REGIONAL DIRECTORS, SUPERINTENDANTS, AND OTHER OFFICIALS, TO KEEP AND SAFELY IMPRISON THE SAID DEFENDANT FRO THE TERM OF SAID SENTENCE IN THE INSTITUTION IN THE STATE CORRECTIONAL SYSTEM TO WHICH YOU, THE SAID DEPARTMENT OF CORRECTIONS, MAY CAUSE THE SAID DEFENDANT TO BE CONVEYED OR THEREAFTER TRANSFERRED. AND THESE PRESENTS SHALL BE YOUR AUTHORITY FOR THE SAME. HEREIN NOT FAIL

WITNESS THE HONORABLE JEREMY PARKER
JUDGE OF THE SAID COURT, AS ALSO CONNIE EVANS
CLERK, AND THE SEAL THEREOF, THIS
24th DAY OF June 20XX-5

BY: Margaret Mills
DEPUTY CLERK

IN THE FIRST JUDICIAL CIRCUIT IN AND FOR
CALUSA COUNTY, STATE OF XXXXX

CIRCUIT CRIMINAL DIVISON

STATE OF XXXXX v. CHARISSA WASHINGTON DEFENDANT	DIVISION: D CASE NUMBER: 20XX(-6)2132

CERTIFICATE OF SERVICE

I, Connie Evans, Clerk of the Circuit Court of the County of Calusa, State of XXXXX, having by law the custody of the seal and all records, books, documents and papers of or appertaining to the Circuit Court, do hereby certify that a true and correct copy of the Judgment and Sentence has been hand delivered to the State Attorney and mailed to the Defense Attorney.

IN WITNESS WHEREOF, I have hereunto set my hand and seal of said Circuit Court, this 24th day of June A.D. 20XX-5.

CONNIE EVANS
As Clerk of Circuit Court

Margaret Mills

As Deputy Clerk
Circuit Criminal Division

IN THE CIRCUIT COURT, 1ST JUDICIAL CIRCUIT
IN AND FOR CALUSA COUNTY, XXXXX
DIVISION : D
CASE NUMBER : 20XX(-6)2132

STATE OF XXXXX
VS
Charissa Washington
DEFENDANT

--------------------------------JUDGMENT--------------------------------

THE DEFENDANT, Charissa Washington, BEING PERSONALLY BEFORE
THIS COURT REPRESENTED WITH
PRIVATE ATTORNEY
Angelia Solomon, Esquire
THE ATTORNEY OF RECORD AND THE STATE REPRESENTED BY ASSISTANT STATE ATTORNEY
George Peabody Smalley, AND HAVING

Been tried and found guilty by a jury of the following crime(s): 1

COUNT	CRIME	STATUTE	COURT ACTION	DATE
1	Possession of a Controlled Substance, to wit, MARIJUANA	80112	GUILTY	16 April 20XX-6

And no cause being shown why the defendant should not be adjudicated guilty, it is ordered that the defendant is hereby adjudicated guilty of the above crime(s).

DEFENDANT Charissa Washington

Division : D

Case Number : 20XX(-6)2132

OBTS Number : 97421119

---SENTENCE---

THE DEFENDANT, BEING PERSONALLY BEFORE THIS COURT, ACCOMPANIED BY THE DEFENDANT'S ATTORNEY OF RECORD, PRIVATE ATTORNEY Angelia Solomon, Esquire

AND HAVING BEEN ADJUDGED GUILTY HEREIN, AND THE COURT HAVING BEEN GIVEN THE DEFENDANT AN OPPORTUNITY TO BE HEARD AND TO OFFER MATTERS IN MITIGATION OF SENTENCE, AND TO SHOW CAUSE WHY THE DEFENDANT SHOULD NOT BE SENTENCED AS PROVIDED BY LAW AND NO CAUSE BEING SHOWN

IT IS THE SENTENCE OF THIS COURT THAT THE DEFENDANT:

Pay a fine of $2000.00, pursuant to appropriate XXXXX Statutes.

Is hereby committed to the custody of the Department of Corrections for a term of: 3 Years, sentence to be suspended pending successful completion of 6 years probation.

-----------------------------------OTHER PROVISIONS-----------------------------------

AS TO COUNT(S) : 1

THE FOLLOWING MANDATORY/MINIMUM PROVISIONS APPLY TO THE SENTENCE IMPOSED :

DEFENDANT Charissa Washington

Division : D

Case Number : 20XX(-6)2132

OBTS Number : 97421119

-----------------------------------OTHER PROVISIONS-----------------------------------

Sentencing guidelines filed.

IN THE EVENT THE ABOVE SENTENCE IS TO THE DEPARTMENT OF CORRECTIONS, THE SHERIFF OF CALUSA COUNTY, XXXXX, IS HEREBY ORDERED AND DIRECTED TO DELIVER THE DEFENDANT TO THE DEPARTMENT OF CORRECTIONS AT THE FACILITY DESIGNATED BY THE DEPARTMENT TOGETHER WITH A COPY OF THIS JUDGMENT AND SENTENCE AND ANY OTHER DOCUMENTS SPECIFIED BY XXXXX STATUTE

THE DEFENDANT IN OPEN COURT WAS ADVISED OF THE RIGHT TO APPEAL FROM THIS SENTENCE BY FILING NOTICE OF APPEAL WITHIN 30 DAYS FROM THIS DATE WITH THE CLERK OF THIS COURT AND THE DEFENDANT'S RIGHT TO THE ASSISTANCE OF COUNSEL IN TAKING THE APPEAL AT THE EXPENSE OF THE STATE SHOWIN OF INDIGENCY.

DONE AND ORDERED IN CALUSA COUNTY, XXXXX, THIS 24TH DAY OF June 20XX-5